DIVE WIGHT AND HAMPSHIRE

A **DIVER** GUIDE

by
MARTIN PRITCHARD
and
KENDALL McDONALD

D1422342

UNDERWATER WORLD PUBLICATIONS LTD

© Copyright 1987
by Underwater World Publications Ltd
55 High Street
Teddington
Middlesex TW11 8HA

Revised 1991

Cover photograph by Les Kemp

Book designed and produced
by Alan Morgan

Maps by Suzanne Blyskal

Typeset in Helvetica by Inhit Ltd trading as Graphic Studios Ltd, 16b High Street, Godalming, Surrey, and printed by Southdown Press, Caxton House, Ham Road, Shoreham-by-Sea, Sussex.

ISBN: 0 946020 15 9

In the same series:

Dive Sussex by Kendall McDonald

Dive Dorset by John & Vicki Hinchcliffe

Dive South Devon by Kendall McDonald and Derek Cockbill

Dive South Cornwall by Richard Larn

Dive West Scotland by Gordon Ridley

Dive North West Scotland by Gordon Ridley

Dive North East by Dave Shaw and Barry Winfield

Dive Yorkshire by Arthur Godfrey and Peter Lassey

Contents

Maps showing the location of dive sites accompany each Area

Advertisers announcements appears on pages 4, 26, 160, 162 and 163

Preface

The coasts of Hampshire and the Isle of Wight can provide some of the most rewarding diving in Britain, but to get the best of it you need expert guidance. That is why the authors have sought out the leading divers in the area and collected together their expertise for inclusion in this book.

Without their help this book could not have been written and so the authors' thanks and those of all the readers of this book go to:

☐ Maurice Harknett of Portsmouth for his great knowledge of Hampshire waters collected during years of diving the area.

☐ Alexander McKee, who found the *Mary Rose,* for telling of many other sites in the Eastern Solent and round the Isle of Wight.

☐ Ray Mabbs, salvage diving expert for much information about wrecks all over the area.

☐ Mike Walsh of Southsea, who has dived professionally all over the world, and who opened his logbooks to provide much diving detail and important transits.

☐ Dougie Saunders of Ryde for immense detail of wrecks all round the Island, particularly the Back of the Wight.

☐ Dave Ellison of Whippingham for diving detail and much photographic research.

☐ Simon Dabell of Blackgang Chine Museum for access to his photographic collections. Tom Rayner of Ryde for more wreck pictures, and Norman Taylor of Gosport for even more.

☐ Paul Davies, skipper of *Seajay,* the dive boat out of Langstone, for help with local wrecks.

☐ The Southern Federation of Sub-Aqua Clubs, the Marine Conservation Society and Jenny Mallinson for permission to draw on that part of their site register for the coast which concerns this book.

☐ The Wight Dolphins, British Sub-Aqua Club Branch No. 807, for a great deal of help with Wight diving.

☐ Lieutenant-Commander J.D. Pugh, R.N. of the Wreck Section of the Hydrographic Department of the Ministry of Defence for all his expertise.

☐ The British Sub-Aqua Club Wreck Register for permission to reproduce some of their wreck marks.

And to all the other divers who helped with their own particular "patch" and their own favourite wrecks.

MARTIN PRITCHARD
KENDALL McDONALD

How to use this book

The coastline of Hampshire and the Isle of Wight is divided into six areas, moving clockwise around the Island. Each area has a chapter to itself containing diving information, spot by spot, wreck by wreck. At the end of each chapter is a section of vital importance to all divers. This contains launch sites, parking places, route information, contact addresses and phone numbers for the local Coastguard, local weather and accommodation. Admiralty chart numbers are given for each area and Ordnance Survey map numbers too. Here you will find details of air supplies, diving boats for hire, outboard service points, equipment sales, hire and repair, and the telephone numbers of the nearest AA 24-hour service centres.

All depths are given in metres. All distances in miles. All dimensions of ships are in feet. Tonnages are gross. Admiralty charts are the metric versions. Ordnance Survey maps are 1:50 000 or about one-and-a-quarter inches to the mile.

Most diving detailed is boat diving, particularly at the Back of the Isle of Wight. Boat diving should be taken to mean inflatable and hard boat diving. This does not mean that all boat diving sites are within inflatable range. No sensible inflatable cox'n would dream of trying to reach some of the sites described. In the same way shore-diving sites are intended only for the strong swimmer on a very calm day.

Each dive site is given a number, which will be found on the area map at the start of each chapter. Please note that in the index the numbers given are site numbers, *not* page numbers.

Divers at Egypt Point (Site 36) during a training session.

Introduction to Hampshire and the Isle of Wight

Some of Britain's best diving is packed into the sea off the coasts of Hampshire and the Isle of Wight. Though the Solent is murky, it is not always so except in the much-boated areas. Visibility to the south of the Isle of Wight is just the opposite. Here the great cliffs, sometimes white, sometimes red, sometimes all the colours of the rainbow, soar up from clear seas and the diving beneath them is just as dramatic.

The waters covered by this book have carried the seaborne traffic of two thousand years in and out of Britain. The commercial port of Southampton and the naval base of Portsmouth have been the destination of many an old-time ship – and these same waters have closed over many a long-lost wreck. Roman pottery has been found in the sea of the Yarmouth Roads, gold coins have been washed up on Isle of Wight beaches, the *Mary Rose* was lost here, and in these waters too, are the wrecks of more modern ships. New discoveries are being made by divers every year. So there is still everything left to dive for! Readers of this book will find over 200 wrecks documented among the dive sites.

Though this book covers the coasts of both Hampshire and the Isle of Wight, they are separated not only by water but also in their administration.

Hampshire is run by Hampshire County Council in Winchester and is the largest non-Metropolitan county in England with a population of over 1.4 million living in an area of 1456 square miles. The southern part of the country is most densely populated, with Portsmouth and Southampton as the main centres and the largest cities in the South-East outside of London. They are two of Britain's major ports and their Naval links go back to the beginning of shipping.

With its mild climate and long coastline – 145 miles – Hampshire is very attractive to divers and other watersports enthusiasts allowing easy access to sheltered waters.

Hampshire's borders were changed in the reorganisation of 1974 and the county now starts in the east just by and including Emsworth and runs to near Highcliffe in the west where Dorset begins.

The Isle of Wight, which likes to call itself "England's Garden Isle", is run by the Isle of Wight County Council based at Newport through two separate borough councils – Medina Borough with Newport, Cowes and Ryde, and South Wight Borough, which includes Sandown, Shanklin, Ventnor and all the rural areas.

The Island has 477 miles of road and about 120,000 residents. The diamond-shaped isle consists of 94,146 acres and is 23 miles long from the

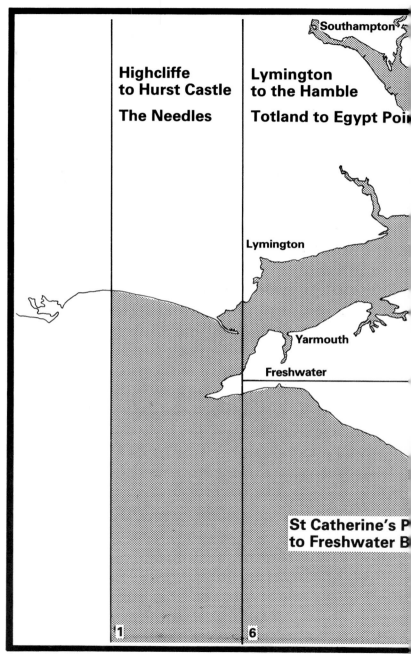

Section Areas

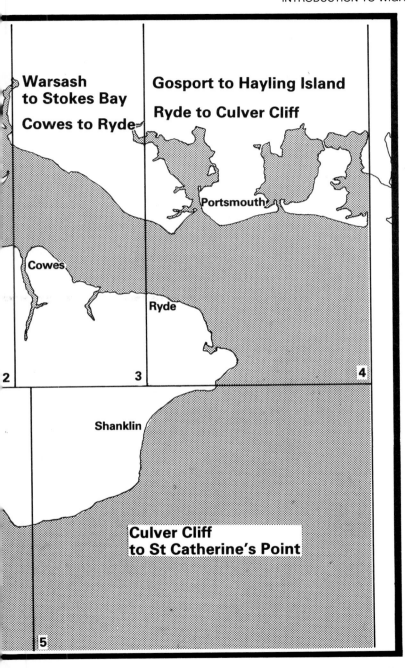

**Warsash
to Stokes Bay**

Cowes to Ryde

Gosport to Hayling Island

Ryde to Culver Cliff

Portsmouth

Cowes

Ryde

2

3

4

Shanklin

**Culver Cliff
to St Catherine's Point**

5

Needles to Bembridge Foreland and 13¼ miles deep from Egypt Point near Cowes to St. Catherine's Point in the south, 155 square miles in all.

The island's climate is mild, apart from occasional arctic abberations, and the coastal scenery is often dramatic and beautiful. The island's motto is "All This Beauty is of God" – and there are 60 miles of coastline for divers to explore.

Access by road

Is easy to Hampshire. Access to the Isle of Wight by car can be difficult at the peak of the holiday season.

Roads to the eastern section of Hampshire are the A3 from Guildford and the A3 Motorway on to the A27 for Portsmouth, or the A32 to Gosport from Alton.

Access to Southampton from the Midlands and North is by the A34 from Oxford. A very fast link runs almost all along the southern part of Hampshire in the shape of the M27. The western end of the Hampshire coast can be reached via the A337 to Lymington.

Departure points for the Isle of Wight car ferries are Portsmouth for Fishbourne, Lymington for Yarmouth, and Southampton for west and east Cowes.

Sealink operate the drive-on-drive-off big ferries from Portsmouth (Gunwharf Road) to Fishbourne. They run every hour with extra sailings every other half-hour at peak times and summer weekends. There is a 2-4 hourly service during the night. Crossing time: 35 mins.

Sealink also operate the Lymington to Yarmouth drive-on-drive-off ferry hourly during the day (half-hourly at peak times and weekends in summer). Crossing time: 30 mins.

Red Funnel operate the services from Southampton to East and West Cowes. Their drive-through ships take one hour for the crossing.

Bookings for Sealink: Sealink Isle of Wight Services, P.O. Box 59, Portsmouth, PO1 2XB. Tel: 0705-827744.

Bookings for Red Funnel: S.a.e. to Car Reservation, Red Funnel Ferries, 12 Bugle Street, Southampton, SO9 4LJ. Tel: 0703-226211.

Taking cars across is not cheap, but a car is essential to travel around the island, especially with diving gear. It is best to book, but it is possible to turn up at the ferry and to cross without too much waiting. Do not delay in booking your return trip. In fact it is sensible to do it before driving away from your port of entry. Mid-week even in high season should not present a problem and the later the crossing the easier it is to embark. The same applies to the really early boats. Fridays, Saturdays and Sundays are naturally the worst.

There are three pedestrian-only routes to the Island. By hydrofoil from Southampton to West Cowes the crossing takes 20 minutes and runs hourly and more frequently in high season. By hovercraft from Southsea to Ryde Esplanade, the service is half-hourly in summer between 9 a.m. and 7 p.m. The crossing takes nine minutes. By high speed catamaran from Portsmouth Harbour Station to Ryde Pier, crossing time is 15 minutes and this service runs between one and three times an hour between 6 a.m. and midnight.

Diver boarding Explorer, *author/diver Pritchard's boat.*

Wrecks

A huge number of wrecks lie in Hampshire and Isle of Wight waters. Few of them, in comparison with many documented losses, have been found or explored by divers. This makes the area of enormous interest to today's wreck hunter.

The most famous of all wrecks in these waters is that of the *Mary Rose,* located by diver Alexander McKee, excavated by teams of British amateur divers, and finally raised to be put on show next to HMS Victory at Portsmouth. There are many earlier ships – or rather traces of them. Divers have found amphora fragments in Yarmouth Roads in such quantity that there must be a wreck of Roman or earlier times buried somewhere in the soft mud of the area. Not far away a bronze gun of the 17th C has been found, together with pewter, but the full wreck site has not yet been uncovered. Four more Roman wrecks are suspected from net recoveries of pottery – all are to the east of the Island.

Very early gold coins have been washed ashore on the Isle of Wight and long narrow ingots of silver of very ancient date have been found by divers. What else lies under the mud of the Solent only divers will find out. Certainly the early trade routes must mean that other ancient ships have been wrecked and long forgotten in these waters where fierce tides, added to violent funnelling winds, can so easily bring disaster to any ship under sail.

The prevailing winds are, like the rest of the Channel, from the south-west, and gales from that direction have driven hundreds of ships to their doom, many on the Back of the Wight. It is here that the Dutch frigate *Juno* was lost in December 1786.

Earlier Dutch East Indiamen found another south-westerly gale laden with doom. The *Campen* was sunk in 1627 trying to get through the Needles into the comparative calm of the Solent away from the storm open sea. The *Campen* was found in 1979 by Northampton BS-AC.

The Northampton divers have found a considerable number of silver coins and other items from that wreck. But the *Campen* was not alone on that October day. There were three other ships with her and two of them actually managed to get *through* the gap in the Needles. The *Campen* did not make it and nor did the *Vliegende Draeck* (Flying Dragon). She ripped her bottom out and sank somewhere in Alum Bay. Some of her was salvaged but divers have yet to discover her remains.

Other ships over the years have reason to hate the Needles where the tide runs at seven knots on Springs. Goose Rock near the lighthouse for example has the wreckage of four ships around it! *HMS Assurance* hit it in 1753, the *Pomone* went down on top of her in 1811, and a schooner called *Dream* added to the seabed tangle in 1837. Divers working on this mass of hardware found under it all 17 Roman coins of 280 A.D!

The wreck diver will find these and 200 other wrecks detailed in this book, that is apart from the wreck list which notes hundreds more! And most of those have yet to be discovered!

At the other end of the Island and nearer the Hampshire shore lie other wrecks of olden times, like *HMS Impregnable,* lost in October 1799, and *HMS Invincible* in 1758. Not far away are ships of much later wars such as *HMS Hazard,* and all around are tank landing craft, submarines, both British and German of both wars, and the steamers which were their victims. It is, you may think, the wreck diver's paradise – and you will not be far wrong! Certainly every year of diving brings new discoveries.

While not seeking to dampen the wreck diver's ardour, it is here that we should give some general words of warning:

In some areas of these waters the seabed is extremely soft and much silting has taken place of even the most modern wrecks, so it is extremely dangerous to enter wrecks without some fool-proof method of return to an exit point. A few fin strokes are enough to turn visibility in and around these silted wrecks to absolute zero.

In poor visibility the tangle or "wreck" net is another great danger to the unwary diver. Though this part of the British coast was not one where wreck netting became extensive, some fishermen have been using these almost invisible modern monofilament nets on sunken ships in the area. Divers must take care on all wrecks as many have trawl and other nets wrapped around them by accident. (See Diving Dangers)

Wreck divers should also make sure that their diving does not offend against the Military Remains Act (See Rules and Regulations).

Rules and regulations

The restrictions on divers in Hampshire and Isle of Wight waters can be split into three main categories – diving in harbours, taking fish or shellfish, and the exploration of Naval ships or military aircraft.

Diving in harbours. This area includes huge ports and busy harbours. Most divers would not want to explore the murky waters of any of them, but those who do must ensure that they have the harbourmaster's permission and must ensure that they dive only in the area for which such permission has been given and only at the times stated. Details of the harbourmasters from whom permission to dive must be sought are listed in each appropriate place in this book.

Taking fish or shellfish. Any diver who wants to take any fish or shellfish for his supper must conform to the same rules as those which apply to professional fishermen. These mostly concern minimum sizes. Such sizes for the whole of our area are laid down by the Southern Sea Fisheries District.

Martin Pritchard with a porthole retrieved from Polo *(Site 170).*

Chief Fishery Officer of this District is Major Tony Parker, generally referred to by local fishermen as "The Major". The Major is no Army man, but very much a sea-going Royal Marine. He is not anti-diver and indeed has great respect for the British Sub-Aqua Club, but is worried about non-members who appear to have caused an upsurge of diver-fisherman incidents lately. Divers should bear this very much in mind when diving sensitive areas.

The Southern Sea Fisheries District is very large and covers the coastline for three nautical miles seaward from the Coastguard Station, Hayling Island, to the Dorset-Devon border and includes the waters around the Isle of Wight, the Solent, Southampton Water, Langstone Harbour, Portsmouth Harbour, Poole Harbour and Portland Harbour. The whole of this District is administered from a head office at 3, Park Road, Poole, Dorset, BH15 2SH. Telephone: Parkstone (0202) 721373. Fisheries officers are also based at Newport, Isle of Wight, and at Gosport.

The District has its own fisheries protection vessel, the 33-foot *Southern Trident,* based at Poole or Cowes. The two skippers, both fisheries officers, divide the area between them. Usually in command when the ship is in the eastern part of the area is Mr. Brian Poore, and in the west Mr. Reg Booth. In addition there are two Searider hard-hulled fast inflatables, one based at Gosport and one at Poole.

Minimum sizes of fish and shellfish laid down by the Southern Sea Fisheries District, at the time of going to press, are as follows:

Fish:

Species	cms	inches
Dab	15	5.9
Sole	24	9.4
Lemon Sole	25	9.8
Megrim	25	9.8
Plaice	25	9.8
Flounder	25.4	10.0
Brill	30	11.8
Turbot	30	11.8
Conger	58	22.8
Skates and rays (between wing tips)	35	13.8
Mullet, Red	17.8	7.0
Herring	20	7.9
Haddock	27	10.6
Whiting	27	10.6
Cod	30	11.8
Hake	30	11.8
Mullet, Grey	30	11.8
Pollack	30	11.8
Bass	32	12.6

Shellfish:

	cms	inches
Crab (Brown) (width at broadest part of back)	14.0	5.5
Crab (Spinous or Spider carapace length)	12.0	4.7
Lobster (carapace length)	8.5	3.4
Oysters (not able to pass through ring, internal diameter)	6.4	2.5
Scallops (Longest part of shell)	10.0	3.9
Mussels (Length)	5.1	2.0
Cockles (not able to pass through square gauge, side)	2.4	15/16ths

N.B. The landing of separate tails of lobsters, and claws of lobsters and crabs, and the taking of soft or spawn-carrying brown or edible crab is prohibited.

These minimum sizes and other details of the Southern Sea Fisheries District regulations are available on a special wheelhouse card sent free to any diver who writes to the Poole H.Q. A copy of the bye-laws is also obtainable from the same address. Southern Fisheries believe that the widest possible distribution of their wheelhouse card is worth more in passing on information than any number of noticeboards.

Diving Naval Wrecks or the wreckage of military aircraft. Here the diver is governed by the Military Remains Act of 1986. The purpose of the Act is to protect the sanctity of "war graves" in the shape of the wrecks of military

The ill-fate HMS Swordfish, *launched at Chatham Dockyard by Lady Tyrwhitt, and now an official war grave (Site 190).*

ships and aircraft known to contain human remains of service personnel. No diver would quarrel with that.

Under the Act the wreckage of all military aircraft of any nation is automatically protected, but Naval ships have to be designated by the Secretary of State, who needs a statutory instrument to do so. This means that ships will have to be named and approved by Parliament in the same way that ships protected as historic wrecks (there are quite a number of these detailed in the waters covered by this book) need a statutory instrument passed through Parliament for each one.

At the time of going to press, a list of designated ships is imminent and divers should watch for details in diving magazines and newspapers. Once ships have been named, the diver commits an offence only if he or she tampers with, damages, moves, removes, or unearths remains, or enters an enclosed interior space in the wreckage. Nothing in the Act prevents the wreck diver from visiting the site, examining the exterior and even settling on the wreckage. An offence is committed only if he disturbs remains or enters a proper compartment in the wreck.

The punishment on conviction of an offence is a fine. It is not clear how the Act will actually work in practice or how proof of an offence could be obtained, particularly in areas where the wreckage of two ships lie side by side or is actually interlocked. Only a brief outline of the main thrust of the Act can be given here, so serious wreck divers should protect themselves by studyying a full copy of the Act, which is obtainable from H.M. Stationery Office Bookshop, 49, High Holborn, London, WC1.

A shoal of pout photographed by Mike Jennings in the wreck of P12 (Site 141).

Marine life

Sandwiched between Sussex and Dorset, this area might be thought to have a marine life that was identical with that of these neighbours, but in fact there are significant differences, though most areas teem with fish and shellfish.

Every wreck in Hampshire and the Isle of Wight area is, like Sussex and Dorset's lost ships, encircled with pouting and pollack. Those on the wrecks further out are of enormous size. Skate, however, are not common and there are many more seen in Sussex and Dorset waters by divers. Another flat fish that is cause for rejoicing when caught by local fishermen is the turbot, also not common. The oyster fishery in the Solent is different. Some stray from recognised beds, being found by divers off Bembridge and round the Forts. Scallops are found in small beds (unlike the big concentrations in Dorset waters) and when found are usually smaller than their western neighbours.

Sole and plaice are common and bass and mullet plentiful. Mackerel are seen in huge shoals. Congers of enormous size haunt the deep wrecks.

Shark, thresher and porbeagles, are known to be in St. Catherine's Race off St. Catherine's Point when they follow the shoals of mackerel up Channel. Gosport, Lymington and Isle of Wight ports all offer the tourists shark-fishing. Sport divers do not appear to have come face to face with the sharks though they have been seen from the big dive boats.

The waters of Hampshire and the Isle of Wight are famous for their crabs, brown as the local fishermen call them and edible by any name!

These crabs, which make up the major part of the fishery in these waters are usually large, with 5-6 lbs being almost standard. Lobsters are common too, and in certain parts of the east end of the area are more prolific than crabs. The Solent is excellent lobster ground, but is not extensively potted due to the amount of shipping traffic. As a result some small wrecks are home to very large specimens.

Dive planning

Weather. If you believe, together with every other diver, that winds only exist to spoil the diving, then you will find the winds in this area particularly annoying. For here winds simply do not behave as they should.

From first glance at a map it would seem certain that the great land mass of the Isle of Wight would protect a great deal of the Hampshire coast from really bad weather. However, it does so only to a certain extent. The protection is far from complete, causing very strange wind effects, as any yachtsman or woman in these waters will tell you. It is quite possible to have yachts sailing up the Solent under spinnackers from both east and west at the same time!

This is the result of "wind bend" when winds from the south-west funnel into the Solent around the Needles from one end, but more of the wind hits the south side of the Island. This wind bounces off the cliffs and literally bends round the great headlands like Culver Cliff until it is coming from almost the opposite direction from which it set out.

However, apart from these tricks the weather of the Hampshire coast and Isle of Wight is not greatly different from that of the rest of Britain – it will change without any warning!

In winter, for example, spells of dull cloudy weather, wet with mild temperatures, can change quickly to brilliant blue skies, but with the temperature down below freezing. And in summer one of those lovely long hot still spells can break almost overnight into chilly, wet and windy weather.

There are certain things about the weather of this area about which you can be sure. One is that the weather to the east is drier than that of the west, where the area known as the Back of the Wight (the "Front" faces the Hampshire coast) collects most of the wind and wet from the south-west.

It is those south-west winds which have accounted over the years for most of the huge number of sailing ship wrecks under the massive cliffs of the "Back".

The holiday resorts on the east of the Island have tucked themselves into the shelter of cliffs out of the wind. It is not surprising that Shanklin has held the British annual sunshine record for more years than any other resort in the country. Even so it is the prevailing south-west air stream which dominates even such sunny areas for long periods in the winter, bringing cloudy and damp conditions with strong winds from December to February.

The following rules about the winds of the area will be of use to the diver cox'n:

When the wind blows down from the Polar regions it arrives from the north-west and brings with it showers and bright periods. Cox'ns should look out for squalls at this time.

Winds from the east and south generally bring warm and dry weather from June to August, but very cold conditions in winter.

Winds from the west are the most frequent throughout the year. Winds from the south-east do not stay long. North-east winds are most likely from March to May.

Gales come most often out of the south-west and west and they usually last from four to six hours in winter, but not so long in the summer. Boathandlers should be warned, however, that just because a gale dies down suddenly, it does not mean that all is over. Whole series of gales have been recorded in the area with wind speeds of over 90 knots, which is more than hurricane force!

Diver-coxn's should know, too, that sea breezes are not always gentle. In fact along the Back of the Wight during warm summer days a sea breeze can combine with the predominant south-westerly and may boost the force by two on the Beaufort Scale between late morning and late afternoon. This can make return to an open beach quite hazardous.

Winds in the area are very subject to funnelling down valleys and off hills. Dive boat skippers should expect wind forces to rise by as much as 20 per cent above the wind speed in surrounding areas at such times. Even some of the main ports of the area are affected by these boosted winds.

All this may sound a little gloomy, but in fact the whole area enjoys a temperature that is higher than average. During the summer the air temperature averages 15°–20° and a mild 8°–12°C for much of the winter.

This means that, on average, the air is colder than the sea from October to March and a bit warmer from April to August. In September there is no difference in temperature between them. At all times the difference between air and sea temperature is small and rarely more than 1°C.

Just as the wind affects diving everywhere, so the wind affects the temperature all round. You can safely say that south-west winds in summer will produce temperatures slightly below average, and in winter will keep things mild. North-west or north-east winds will do nothing much to summer warmth, but will give you cold weather in winter. East and south winds will give really warm weather in summer, but produce a very cold winter nip.

As well as sensing the wind, the diver-cox'n ought to be keeping his eyes on the clouds. When big cumulo-nimbus clouds appear it may well be time to batten down the hatches – squally showers and hail with thunder can appear very suddenly. This, coupled with a swift change in wind direction and a sudden increase in wind speed, can put a small boat or inflatable at risk.

Thunderstorms generally develop over France and drift north across the Channel during the night. The sudden squalls which come with them seem to be tied in some way with the appearance of solitary watersprouts.

Snow and sleet will be of interest only to the all-seasons diver, but they may like to know that these appear most between January and March and the average frequency for this area is two days per month between those dates. If you are thinking of such cold diving, ice can form in shallow waters to the east of the area in very severe winters. In January 1963 ice in the harbours of Fishbourne and Lymington interrupted the ferries across the Solent.

Fog, particularly in summer, can affect all divers and is particularly worrying at sea for the dive-boat skipper with divers down when the fog banks start to roll in. They do appear very suddenly. In south-west wind conditions extensive banks may form at any time of year. Sea fog is most likely when the wind veers westerly and it is most common in spring and summer because of the mild westerlies blowing over colder waters. These fogs can persist for two or three days, but are unlikely to last more than six hours. The risk of sea fog declines from May and June when on average three fogs occur to an average of one only in August and September.

Tides. Tidal streams through the English Channel are fairly straightforward. They run to the east for the flood tide and to the west on the ebb. The strength of the streams vary with the width of the Channel, running stronger in the narrow parts and weaker in the wide.

Island diver Dougie Saunders with the port lamp he retrieved from HMS Boxer (Site 151).

This simple truth becomes complicated when one starts to deal with tidal currents and streams in the area around the Isle of Wight. The western part of the English Channel is wide and as a result the tides are not particularly strong. But as you come up Channel to the east and approach the waters of the Island the width of the Channel narrows dramatically with the distance between the Isle of Wight and the Cherbourg Peninsula coming down to a mere 55 miles. Then tidal streams speed up and Springs can reach three-and-a-half knots.

With tidal streams running both east and west around the Isle of Wight into the Solent then strange tidal patterns emerge. Most Solent ports and harbours experience a double High Water with the flood tide running in two stages separated by a period of near slack water. The flood runs for about seven-and-a-half hours and the ebb for five-and-a-quarter.

Generally, the ebb tides will be stronger than the flood as the water which took seven-and-a-half hours to come in only has five-and-a-quarter hours to get out. The ebb also picks up speed quicker than the flood and this must be taken into account when diving on High Water slacks.

In the area, too, are several prominent headlands and deep narrow channels and tidal streams always run more strongly in these areas. Beware of inshore eddies where the tide may turn much earlier than the main stream. In the Solent these eddies are particularly prominent and are sought after by yachts racing against a foul tide. They can be seen quite clearly from a diving boat – there is a "tide line" about six feet wide, full of assorted debris and floating weed between the two steams.

Tidal heights range between 3.5m at High Water on Neaps and 5.1m on Spring High Water above chart datum.

Visiting divers have been swept away from their dive sites and travelled a considerable distance before being picked up. They do not appear to have anticipated the strength of local tides. The golden rule for "Diving Wight" is to arrive on site early and wait for slacks to reach you. On offshore sites and wrecks, it is best not to anchor the dive boat, but to mark the site with a shot line and keep the boat free to pick up any divers who may be swept off the target.

More detailed tidal advice for each area in this book will be found in the introduction to each section. Tidal information is based on the time of High

Water at Portsmouth. The time of slack water has been averaged, but remember it can vary with the strength of the tide and local weather conditions.

Visibility. Some divers say that the visibility in the Solent is always so bad that there is never any point in diving there. They are wrong. The truth is that the viz varies considerably throughout the area, but is worse in the places where the seabed is muddy and the tidal streams run at their strongest. In areas of rock and low tidal movement the visibility is bound to be at its best.

As a general rule, visibility will be better during periods of Neap tides and during periods of dry settled weather. Strong onshore winds will reduce the visibility inshore of the 10m depth line very quickly indeed.

Though the viz varies from day to day, divers should find the following simple area by area guide of use in their general dive planning:

Area 1. In the open water parts of this area visibility is usually good. The average is from 5-7m. On occasions it will exceed 10m. Through the Needles Channel the best visibility is usually found around High Water and can reach 6-7m. This reduces as the ebb tide starts to run out of the Western Solent.

Area 2. Throughout the Western Solent the best visibility will normally be found in the shallower parts averaging between 2-4m. In the deeper waters of the main channel it will only rarely exceed 2m.

Area 3. Central Solent viz is much the same as Area 2. It will normally improve to the east of the area.

Area 4. Visibility usually improves quickly as the murky waters of the Solent are left behind. Off Portsmouth and around the Solent Forts it will be between 3-4m. Further south off Bembridge Ledges it can reach 5-6m.

Area 5. Average summer viz is around 5-7m, reaching 6-10m further to the south. There are recognised dumping grounds to the east of this area and visibility in the immediate vicinity will decrease drastically when they are in use.

Area 6. Summer visibility will usually be in the region of 6-10m. Inshore of the Back of the Wight, strong onshore winds will stir up the sand over the Brook and Atherfield Ledges and reduce the viz to zero. After a strong blow the shape and extent of the ledges can be seen very easily by looking down from the top of the cliffs when they are marked by the sandy-coloured water over them.

Navigation. Diver cox'ns should note carefully certain points about handling boats in the area. For example, buoyage in the area follows the normal convention of red to port and green to starboard – with one exception. Within the Eastern Solent the opposite applies – red port hand are on the Island side and green starboard are on the Hampshire side.

It hardly needs saying that the area is heavily used by shipping of all kinds, but it does need saying that no diver can be too careful in this area of deep channels and narrows. Once in them many ships cannot alter course due to their deep draught and are quite unable to reduce speed quickly or to travel at very low speeds due to the loss of steerage. Divers must not get in their way!

Areas where the greatest care is needed are off the Needles between the

Needles Bridge Buoy and the south-west Shingles Buoy and in the deep water channels of both the Eastern and Western Solent.

Off Cowes ships inward-bound to Southampton from the east turn to the south after passing the Prince Consort Buoy, then arc to the north to enter the Thorn Channel. Once this turn has started it must continue so keep well away from big ships turning in this area (See Area 3).

Another area for great vigilance is the channel and entrance to Portsmouth. Big ferries and naval ships are coming and going all the time. Small boats must use the designated small-boat channel through the entrance. Many ferries after leaving Portsmouth head south-east until they reach the Bembridge Ledge Buoy where they turn to the south-west to pass inshore of the Princessa Buoy on the west side of the Princessa Shoal. The reverse procedure is adopted when they are in-bound for Portsmouth, so keep a good lookout for them when diving in the locality.

In the area between Stone Point and Lepe on the Hampshire coast, and between Egypt Point and Thorness Bay on the Island, there are high voltage cables and gas pipelines running across the Solent. Anchoring of any kind is forbidden in this area.

During the summer months large spherical yellow buoys blossom in Solent waters. They bear names such as Deck, Frigate, Keel, Ratsey, Porsche and so on. They are, of course, marker buoys for yacht racing – if diving nearby remember you have been warned!

While on the subject of yachts – in June each year the Round The Island race attracts an entry in excess of 1200 boats. They race from Cowes, heading west and circling the Island to finish at Cowes again. This is a day the Solent and Wight diver might think would be better spent in a pub! The first week in August is Cowes Week and a time when the Solent and other areas are packed with yachts. Though we have nothing against "yotties", it is a time when divers might well take avoiding action!

Diving dangers

Divers and fishing nets. So far no diver has been reported as trapped in tangle nets in Hampshire or Isle of Wight waters, though this may be more a matter of luck than of any other significance. Certainly divers only a few miles away in Dorset waters have been caught up in these wreck nets and have been lucky to escape with their lives.

Wreck netting has not caught on so widely in Hampshire seas and around the Island as it has elsewhere and the Southern Sea Fisheries describe the use of such nets as "not a major feature of the fishing effort". This must not be taken to mean that no wreck netting takes place. It does, and divers should be on the alert for these almost invisible killers on every wreck they dive.

The modern tangle and gill net is made of a monofilament material, which is extremely difficult to see, hence its increased effectiveness over the older type of net whose knots stood out in even poor visibility. These nets are different from those of trawlers, which often become draped on wrecks by accident. It is only in very recent years that nets have been deliberately placed on wrecks.

These tangle nets are known to fishermen as "wreck nets" and their use, in most of British waters, grew swiftly, until some sort of stability was reached in 1986. The nets used are usually about 53m long with floats at one metre intervals. The bottom of the net is attached to a footrope weighted with galvanised steel rings. The footrope is designed to break so that the net can be torn free if totally snagged on the wreck.

This netting is generally for pollack, conger and sometimes cod, in fact any other large fish which congregate around wrecks. Wrecks are usually fished on neap tides only and are left netted for 24 hours before being hauled. This means that there may be no sign of life when the dive boat arrives at the wreck and indeed the marker float may be submerged. (The fishing boat will have no difficulty in relocating the wreck and the nets with modern electronic gear.) The need for care is obvious. Wreck nets are usually laid in a fleet of three to five straddling the wreck.

The danger to divers is not only on wrecks. Nets are often set for bass. Since 1978 an important fishery for bass, which fetch extremely high prices, has grown up inshore between Selsey Bill and Swanage using monofilament gill nets. Main concentration of this fishery is in the Solent and Southampton Water. In addition to the real full-time professional fishermen, large numbers of part time, casual and amateur fishermen are using gill nets. One estimate is that in the area, 100,000 of nets are laid by them. Even a small boat can carry a huge length of net.

Set nets are also used close inshore for plaice and sole, a major part of the catch for the area, but the majority of the Solent sole catch is by trawling.

It is clear that in the area there is an enormous amount of net about and divers must be alert at all times. Worried about the threat of nets to the diver's safety, the British Sub-Aqua Club carried out special tests, deliberately entangling divers in this type of modern monafilament net. As a result their advice is to carry a small special knife or a pair of small stainless steel shears. They found that the standard large diver's knife was ineffective, regardless of how sharp it had been kept.

The diver and gear underwater present a multitude of points on which net can become snagged. A survey showed that the majority of divers who had become entangled, had got caught first on their legs. Despite this divers tend to wear their knives on their legs and present a major snagging point. It would be better if a small knife or small shears were worn on the arm or in an easily accessible purpose-made pocket on the upper part of the suit or lifejacket.

If a diver does become entangled, the BS-AC advise partial inflation of the lifejacket making the diver rise inside the net, pulling it under tension and making it easier to cut. They say that the positive buoyancy will also help to tear the diver free. If your buddy is clear of the netting he should cut you out still emeshed and finish the clearance on the surface.

Decompression accidents

The procedure to be followed if these occur is laid down in the Safe Diving Practices leaflet compiled by the National Diving Committee of the British Sub-Aqua Club. This says:

"Decompression sickness symptoms vary between those so sudden that immediate air evacuation to a chamber is vital, to those which may not become apparent for some hours. Some of these less dramatic symptoms, which may well be delayed, can be more serious and produce greater disability than the excruciating pain associated with a

Divers and "White P". Divers exploring the wrecks of World War One vintage in this area should be aware that "wedges" of phosphorus are being found in increasing numbers on these ships. One very good description of them is that they look like "wedges of Danish blue cheese – just like you see in a supermarket". Divers should avoid handling these "wedges" (or sticks), which ignite spontaneously when exposed to air – one woman diver was burned after bringing up a stick of this white waxy substance and putting it in her pocket! This white phosphorus was produced for the Allies in the First World War by one Midlands firm, whose output for the whole war was 6083 tons. "White P" was used in a wide variety of munitions – for incendiary shells; for thermalite and phosphorus grenades, trench mortar bombs, a whole range of shells, and 12-pounder aircraft bombs and for 6-inch, 4-inch, and 3-inch naval shells, both incendiary and shrapnel.

"White P" can look yellowy and almost veined like cheese and comes in various shapes. Those seen so far are either "wedges" or little sticks. But whether it is cheese-shaped or looks like a fish finger, divers should treat it all the same way – don't touch it, don't bring it up. It not only burns, it is also deadly poisonous.

Depth. Many wrecks in the area are deep and in some places are dark as well. Divers should remember that 50m is the recommended depth for sport diving. In their booklet "Safe Diving Practices", the National Diving Committee of the British Sub-Aqua Club draw attention to the fact that there is medical evidence that decompression sickness is more likely to occur on dives deeper than 50m, even though the tables are strictly adhered to. Such occurrences are usually extremely serious.

They say that there is strong evidence too, particularly with the onset of nitrogen narcosis, that 40m ought to be the maximum depth to which most divers should dive. The National Diving Committee add that when diving deeper than 30m, special care is vital and strongly recommend that dives in excess of 50m should not be undertaken by sports divers.

joint bend. Tingling and numbness are included in this category. The procedures for dealing with such a range of symptoms depend on the timing of their onset and the geographical location of the subject."

At sea: "Air embolism or severe Type 2 Bend symptoms, occurring at sea, requires rapid transfer of the subject to a recompression chamber, with their legs elevated and, if possible, the administration of 100 per cent oxygen. Being bounced, rapidly, in a small boat is almost certainly going to worsen the symptoms rather than help the situation. RAF Search and Rescue helicopters will almost certainly be involved and the use of VHF radio is essential.

"HM Coastguard, although co-ordinating all rescues at sea, are not medically qualified to diagnose diving-related medical disorders and have to seek advice before activating a 'Medivac' air evacuation. The Department of Transport and British Telecom International operate a Radio Medical Advisory Service through the BTI Coast Radio Stations.

Members of Enfield BS-AC relaxing on board Explorer *after a dive.*

"If your radio has a 'Duplex' operating system, with Coast Radio Station working frequencies, it is advisable to contact the nearest Coast Radio Station where you will be put in direct contact with a doctor, via a telephone link. There is no charge for this service. Once the doctor has given his advice, the Coastguard is in a position to follow up without delay.

"If your radio does not have Coast Radio Station frequencies, or has a 'Simplex' operating system, it is advisable to contact the Coastguard on Channel 16.

"This may take more time, as the Coastguard will have to contact the doctor on your behalf. If the situation is serious enough a 'Pan-Pan' call would be necessary."

On land. "If decompression sickness symptoms arise on land and they are serious, you are advised to dial 999 and ask for an ambulance, explaining the symptoms on the phone. If a helicopter is needed, the doctor will contact the Coastguard (if you are on the coast) who will co-ordinate the rescue. Inland, rapid transport with police escort, can be arranged by the medical emergency services.

"With less dramatic symptoms, contact with a GP or hospital casualty department is advisable. Ensure you carry the HMS *Vernon* phone number – 0705 818888 and ask for the Duty Diving Medical Specialist or Duty Lieutenant Commander – to enable the doctor concerned to get specialist medical advice. Transfer to the nearest available recompression chamber, where necessary, will be arranged."

Divers and Pot Fishermen

The major fishery in the area is for "brown" or edible crab and these are obtained by boats of all shapes and sizes and a fishing effort ranging in scale from the single pot to strings of well over 50 at a time.

Unlike the neighbouring fisheries district, Sussex, the Southern Sea Fisheries District, which covers Dorset as well as Hampshire and the Isle of Wight, puts no limits on the number of pots per professional registered fishing boat. Some of the larger boats set their pots in mid-Channel and then land their catch in France. On the return trip they pick up another catch from the re-baited pots and land that in Britain and alternate in this way on each voyage. At least nine registered in Hampshire fish right outside the fisheries limits.

Area landings of all fish in 1985 for West Hampshire was 1,400 tons, for East Hampshire 995 tons, and for the Isle of Wight 236 tons. Of this 1,119 tons were of edible crab. Lobster landings were much smaller at 115 tons, but were the bigger money spinners for most fishermen. This is liable to make the area one of sensitivity as far as diver-fishermen relations are concerned. Until recently and since a flare-up in the 1970's diver-fisherman relations have been extremely good. In fact in the Isle of Wight there has never been any trouble and conflict between diver and fisherman is not only unknown but quite the reverse is true.

However, Major Tony Parker chief of the Southern Sea Fisheries District (See Rules and Regulations) says that recently in other areas there have been a number of incidents. Major Parker has a great respect for the British Sub-Aqua Club and the work they have done in this sensitive field. He worries about those divers who are not Club members. He understands about the diver's need to explore rocky areas and that in doing so the diver will inevitably come close to pot markers without ever having touched the pots. But he feels that some "cowboys" have stolen from pots, and believes that some fishermen's complaints are justified. So divers should bear all this in mind when diving in the area and take every precaution to stay clear of fishermen's gear. Remember fish landings in the district are getting on for £1,000,000 in value per year and this makes the situation very volatile. Shellfish landings are made at many places, but are generally channelled through Portsmouth on the mainland or Bembridge or Wootton on the Island.

Helping to keep the good relations which generally exist between divers and fishermen and local people is the Southern Federation of Sub-Aqua Clubs. They will sort out any problems encountered by visiting divers or local people. Expert in this area over many years is Southfed's Chairman Dr. Ken Collins, 2, New Cottages, Lower Brownhill Road, Millbrook, Southampton, SO1 9LL. Tel: Southampton (0703) 783710. He will be happy to advise any divers who contact him.

BS-AC coach for the area covered by this book is the Southern Regional Coach Tony Cummings, 59 King Edward Avenue, Moordown, Bournemouth, Dorset BH9 1TZ. Tel: (0202) 528390. Tony will be happy to sort out any problems concerning diving in the area and is a good source of information about diving Hampshire and the Isle of Wight.

Area 1: Highcliffe to Hurst Castle and the Needles

This area runs from 01 41 00 to 01 33 00 and stretched right down to the foot of Chart No. 2045. It takes in a graveyard of lost ships and particularly those close to the chalk spikes of the Needles. It is here that the entry to the Western Solent is at its most dangerous and many sailing ships, driven by south-westerlies, never made the entrance. Some ended up on the huge cliffs of the Back of the Wight; others were swallowed up by the Shingles, those great shifting banks of pebbles which stretch diagonally across the obvious route in to the Solent.

This whole area can be a difficult one for divers and it is important for them to understand the tidal patterns, which vary dramatically from one part of the area to the other.

The northern half, for example, produces very strong tidal streams. At the narrow entrance to the Solent between Hurst Castle on the Hampshire side and Fort Albert on the Isle of Wight – the narrowest part of the whole Solent – the flood tide runs in a north-easterly direction and can reach speeds of 4 knots. The ebb runs south-west and can go even faster – up to nearly 5 knots.

It is surprisingly deep in the narrow straits, reaching over 60m very close in. Despite the depth there is often a great tumult on the surface. Much of this is caused by a strong stream running through the North Channel (between the Hampshire coast and the northern edge of the Shingles). Through here the flood tide reached 3-3½ knots in the deeper parts. Its speed increases as it reaches Hurst Castle and, where it finally joins the Needles Channel stream about 400 yards south of Hurst Castle, violent eddies are often created.

But on the ebb tide this main stream branches off at Hurst Castle where some runs through the North Channel to disperse into Christchurch Bay and the rest goes down through the Needles Channel into open water. On the ebb this movement causes a strong inshore eddy along the Hampshire coastline.

Off the Needles themselves and the Lighthouse, the flood tide reaches 2½ knots and the ebb slightly more – up to 3 knots. Across the Needles Bridge rocks, when the streams are strong and full, a line of disturbed sea is clear to see. This disturbed area goes completely mad when a strong westerly wind blows against an ebbing tide and then the seas can truly be described as mountainous.

The Shingles cover a large area stretching from a little south of Hurst Castle down as far as the Needles Bridge Buoy. These shingle banks are well marked by buoys. Although it is a shallow area, the tidal streams still

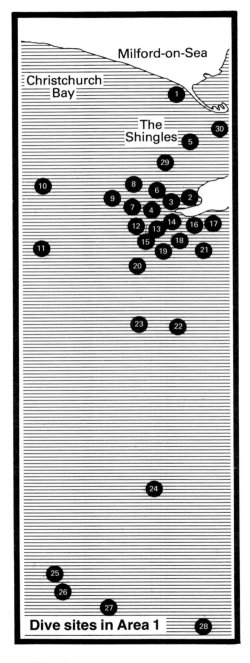

Dive sites in Area 1

run across them strongly and there always seems to be disturbed water over them. The banks are constantly shifting and at Low Water Springs parts of them are exposed. The ebb tide running against a strong westerly wind will produce some spectacular and breaking seas and obviously great care must be taken by any small boat.

Slack water in this area occurs about one hour before High Water and five hours after High Water Portsmouth and the slack lasts only for 10-20 minutes depending on whether Spring or Neap.

In the southern half of the area, well south of the western end of the Isle of Wight, the east-going stream can reach 2½ knots and the west-going about 3 knots. The general depths are between 30-40m and slack water comes one hour before High Water and five hours after High Water Portsmouth. Here the slack period lasts for 15-45 minutes once again dependent on Neap or Springs.

As far as the Hampshire coastline is concerned there is little diving from the shore, though some do go off the single spit running out to Hurst Castle in search of flatfish. The real diving in the area is all boat diving, with the exception of Alum Bay. (See Site No. 2). The small boat launch sites for this area are all on the Hampshire side.

Launch sites

Along the Hampshire coast from the Dorset border near the famous luxury hotel of Chewton Glen the A337 comes first to Barton, where, though there is a magnificent car park, access to the sea is confined almost entirely to board sailing.

Milford-on-Sea is the first small boat launch site. Right on the front, with a magnificent view of the Needles and Hurst Castle, is a good car park. A tiny lift over a low wall and across a shingle beach will get the boat into the water. The shingle bank here can be steep.

Keyhaven, further to the east, provides even better launching from a good concrete slip right in front of Keyhaven Yacht Club. This ramp is useable by inflatables at all states of the tide except very low Springs. Many speed boats with big outboards have come to grief within seconds of launching here as the cox'n opened up and headed for the widest part of the channel. The left-hand side of the channel facing the sea is in fact the shallowest side with sandbanks. So keep to the right-hand side. Fishing boats in the area take sole and bass. Parking for car and trailer is close by. This is a public launching site.

Shore diving sites (Hampshire):

1 Hurst Castle Spit. This huge bank of pebbles runs out from the Milford shore for a mile and a half, reaching almost half-way to the Isle of Wight. Though there is no exact point for this shore dive, those who find it interesting – for plaice – say that the further along the Spit you carry your gear the better the dive, but most tend to go only a short way out along the barren pebble ridge. In places stone has been dumped to stop the Spit being breached and the flooding of the marshes to the east. This has happened in the past. Divers anywhere in this area *must* be well aware of the vastly powerful tides which sweep through the Solent at its narrowest point. The closer to Hurst Castle – built by Henry VIII and famous as the prison of Charles I in 1648 – the stronger the tides.

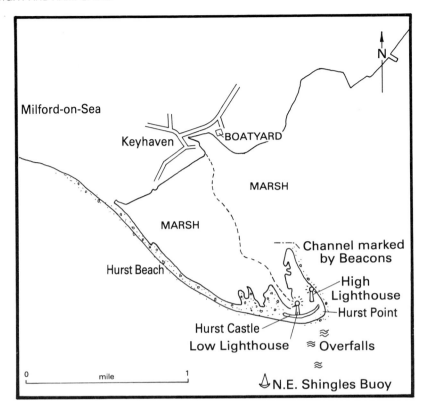

Hurst Point has two lighthouses. Hurst Point Low Lighthouse is 16m high with a red square tower and is sited on the Castle. Hurst Point High Lighthouse has a white round tower and is 26m tall. It is 250 yards behind the Low Lighthouse.

Shore diving sites (Isle of Wight):

2 Alum Bay. This attractive bay lies between Needles Point and Hatherwood Point about a mile to the north-east. The Bay is famous for its cliffs of many colours on the east side and these multi-coloured sands are bottled and sold as souvenirs. Beach diving is possible. Two pylons support a chairlift down to the beach some 400 yards south of Hatherwood Point. Unless you fancy a long hike down a wooden stairway from the car park at the top of the cliff, the chairlift is the beach diver's best method of getting himself and his gear down.

Alum Bay Pier Wreck. The remains of an old sailing vessel provide some life. The depth here is very shallow, less than five metres. The wooden hull is covered with kelp.

The Tool Wreck. Not far from the remains of the old pier. The 50-foot vessel was called Enid. The wreckage of this wooden ship is only a few yards offshore at the extreme southern end of the beach. Many timbers stick up out of the sand. This MFV was wrecked here in a storm a few years ago. Divers have been surprised at the number of tools and electric drills they found among the wreckage, which lies on sand in 5m. Her cargo appears to have included cutlery judging by the amount around the site. The whole seabed of this bay is sand and shingle, but this gives way to rock and weed further out. Maximum depth in the bay is 10m.

The Long Rock. This rock, which dries, lies in the middle of the bay and in the centre of an area of foul ground which often has only two metres of water over it. The main rock area runs for 300 yards to the west of the rock. There is some shellfish life, though there are no reports of anything large. Boat cover is needed.

Five Fingers Rock. This feature is said to have five rock ridges running 300 yards out from it. The main rock lies the same distance to the south-west of Hatherwood Point. It does not dry but is very shallow, and at Low Springs it can have less than a metre of water over it. Much weed and small marine life abound.

Boat diving sites

3 Alum Bay South. This is the area just inside Needles Point and is the best of the diving. A boat is essential and it is not a dive which can be attempted from the beach at Alum Bay. The dive is along the ridges and gullies at the foot of the huge chalk cliffs right at the southern end of the bay. One particularly good patch is just 400 yards north-east of Needle Point itself where the rocks come to within 5m of the surface. This and the gullies under the cliffs are the home of big plaice and big shellfish. There are one or two small wooden wrecks here and a deal of debris. Divers will see many bass hereabouts. Because of their presence some of the boats specialising in bass fishing will come right in to very shallow water. Diver-cox'ns have been warned! The area is generally sheltered. Depths go down to 15m.

4 The Needles. A landmark — and seamark — and one that it is almost impossible to mistake for anything else. The Needles are all that is left of a chalk ridge which centuries ago ran without a break to the Old Harry Rocks just north of Swanage. A change of sea levels let the sea smash through the ridge to flood the old Solent River valley and form the Solent more or less as we know it today.

The Needles today are a narrow chalk peninsula rising up from the rocks to over 400 feet. They too are not the same as they were. In fact the spike which really gave them their name disappeared over 200 years ago. There were five prominent stacks, one of which was joined to the mainland by an arch. The arch collapsed around the time of the Battle of Waterloo. The chalk has always been eroded by the sea as it is today and probably will be for ever. It was erosion which caused the collapse of the very slender pinnacle which is believed to have given the Needles their name. This "needle" was 115 feet high and stood slightly to the north of the main group. Locally it was called "Lot's Wife" and it fell into the sea in 1764.

The Needles have often been a welcoming sight for those homeward-bound. For others they have been a cause of great fear and for some the last sight they have seen. For they are more than just great white portals to the Solent standing out from the dark ground behind them. The rocks at their feet extend a further 400 yards to the west of Needles Point and then the Needles Bridge, a deadly reef with depths varying from 2m to 8m over it, extends well over a mile to the west again. This reef is clearly marked by overfalls in rough weather and in flat calm there are still ripples to be seen – except at complete slack water.

The Needles Lighthouse. Many ships have been lost on the Needles Bridge in addition to those driven into the actual Needles. And the rocks in the area have always been a hazard to shipping both into and out from Portsmouth and Southampton.

As long ago as 1781 merchants and shipowners petitioned Trinity House for a lighthouse. In January 1782 it seemed they were to get their wish. A light was to be erected "to be kept burning in the nightseason whereby seafaring men and mariners might take notice and avoid danger . . . and that ships and other vessels of war might safely cruise during the nightseason in the British Channel". However it was not until 1785 that Trinity House started work on the lighthouse and it first sprang into light on September 29, 1786. It did not work well. The tower had been erected on the top of a cliff overlooking Scratchell's Bay and was some 474 feet above the sea. At that height the light was often shrouded in sea mist and fog.

In 1859, a new lighthouse was built on the outermost point of the chalk rocks and near sea level. Designed by James Walker, it cost £20,000. The base was stepped unevenly to break the force of the waves. Much of the rock at the base was cut away in building the foundations. This made it possible for cellars and storehouses under the lighthouse to be excavated from the chalk. The lighthouse is a circular granite tower standing 108 feet high and its 35,000 candle-power light, nearly 80 feet above the sea, has a range of 17 miles. The lighthouse, with its distinctive red band and red lantern and gallery standing out against the white chalk background, is manned by a principal keeper and two assistants. The light is a white, red and green grouping occulting twice every 20 seconds. The fog signal sounds twice every 30 seconds.

Diving the Needles needs good weather. Even in moderate winds there can be a very uncomfortable swell around the rocks and particularly over the Bridge. Wind against tide is, of course, even worse. Divers must be aware that tides over the Bridge can reach speeds of up to 5 knots and that slack water periods are very short – only 20 minutes on Neap tides.

Average depths over the Bridge are 10-15m and the seabed is almost entirely rock. The Bridge is a favourite area for angling boats and the diver-cox'n should expect to see anglers in the area during any times when diving is possible.

Diving behind the shelter of the large white rocks of the Needles themselves is usually possible at any time, but though the tide run is greatly diminished a nasty swell can build up in the shallow waters close in to the rocks where the depth is only 4-5m. The seabed here is chalky rock with sand and shingle patches.

Scratchell's Bay is the name of the small area between the Needles Lighthouse and Sun Corner, half a mile to the south-east. St. Anthony's Rock stands half-a-metre high at Low Springs 200 yards to the west of the point of Sun Corner and another 200 yards to the west two other rocks will be just awash at the same time. In the Bay are the remains of the wreck of the *Irex*. (See Site 17). Access is by boat only.

A calm view of the Needles lighthouse, marking a hazardous area for shipping, only to be dived in good weather.

The Shingles. This is a series of banks – or perhaps just one great bank – of shingle, sand and gravel which forms the north-west side of the Needles Channel. Tides are tricky (see tidal information in the introduction to this area). The north-west side of the Shingles slopes gradually down to 25m, but the south-east side of the bank is very steep racing up to only ten metres from 30 metres and looking in places like a hanging wall of shingle just about to topple down into the depths.

It is also a ship-swallower and whole ships have been known to disappear into it only shortly after being wrecked. But the Shingles move and the ships do tend to emerge from time to time. The *Iron Ship* (See site 5) is a good example.

Parts of the Shingles dry at times of Low Springs and can show as much as 2m above water. There are many other patches which at the same time will only just be covered. Southerly gales are the ones which really set the banks on the move. The general drift is to the south-west.

Diver-cox'ns must take great care wherever they are on the Shingles. Overfalls appear suddenly on the south-east side on the flood and during the ebb a short sea can appear on the northern edge.

5 Iron Ship At 50 41 33; 01 34 21. Depth: 7m. This wreck was located by divers clearing some fishing nets after they had snagged on the edge of the Shingles Bank in 1983. The site lies on the Needles Channel side of the banks just one and a quarter miles south-west of Hurst Point.

The nets were found to be entangled in the wreck of some sort of coaster or barge, probably fairly old as there is evidence that it was steam powered. The wreck is around 200ft long with a 30ft beam and lies in an east-west direction. The bows appear to have either sunk into the shingle or have disappeared altogether into deeper water. Within the wreck are many copper pipes and the remains of her cargo which appears to have been

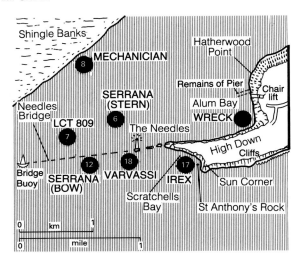

iron pyrites. The divers estimated that the wreck was from the 1890-1914 period, and is only now emerging from the shingle.

Yarmouth 3 miles; Lymington 4 miles.

6 Serrana. This is the stern of the vessel. At 50 39 53; 01 35 41. Depth: 20m. For details of the loss of the *Serrana,* see Site 12. This section is just half-a-mile away from the bows and is spread over an area of about 200ft. Though almost completely broken it appears to be lying on the starboard side with some plates and ribs sticking up some 2 or 3m. The site runs north to south with the stern to the north. The seabed is sand and shingle with a few rocky outcrops. One of these is quite confusing to echo-sounders. It is a red sandstone needle jutting straight up from the seabed to a height of five metres, and it is close to but not in the wreckage. Until recently a 14ft diameter iron propellor lay across some of the wreck at the northern end.

Yarmouth 4.5 miles; Lymington 6 miles.

7 LCT 809. At 50 39 42; 01 36 24. Depth: 20m. This is the remains of the 611-ton tank landing craft No. 809, which was lost a quarter of a mile north-west of the Needles while en route to the Normandy beaches during Operation Neptune in June, 1944. She was built in July 1943 by A. Findlay and Company of Old Kilpatrick, Scotland, and measured 187ft by 39 by 4ft. Dispersal operations took place during 1959. These have left the majority of the wreck standing less than a metre high and very well broken. There is a bit of a mystery about the wreck. When dived by professional diver Mike Walsh of Southsea, he found some bronze steam parts in the wreckage. It is hardly likely that these came from the landing craft, but their origin is unknown. *Warning:* Strong tides make this a difficult dive.

Yarmouth is 5 miles; Lymington 7 miles.

8 Mechanician. At 50 40 13; 01 36 20. Depth: 10m. It took two torpedoes from Kurt Stöter's *UB-35* to sink this big armed escort vessel of 9044 tons.

He hit her first 8 miles west of St. Catherine's Point on January 20, 1918, but even after his two torpedoes went home she still staggered on until she finally grounded on the edge of The Shingles at the entrance to the Needles Channel with 13 men dead aboard. There she was abandoned and by October that year was a total wreck and in two separate halves. Later still the shingle closed over much of her.

Nor did Stöter and *UB-35* last long either. A week after he had attacked the *Mechanician,* on January 26, he was depth-charged and sunk by the destroyer *Leven* in the Dover Straits. None of the crew survived the depth-charging, but six did survive from her crew – they had been on board the Greek steamer *Epstatios* the day before as a boarding party from *UB-35,* when a Navy patrol boat appeared, drove off the submarine and took the German sailors of the boarding party prisoner.

The *Mechanician* was 482ft long with a beam of 57ft. She drew 31ft. Today parts of her are just three metres clear of the shingle, though it is obvious that most of her is buried. The edge of the shingle bank here moves from time to time and some divers see more than others because of that.

Professional diver Mike Walsh located her after getting a strong magnetometer reading "When we dived, there was little to see – most of the wreck is buried in the shingle with only isolated parts sticking up through it," he says.

It is a site worth checking after a good blow.

Yarmouth 5 miles; Lymington 6 miles.

9 Concrete barge. At 50 39 39; 01 37 18. Depth 10m. This wreck is a concrete barge, around 70ft long, which sank while under tow of the motor tug *Pullwell,* on January 19, 1980.

She lies in shallow water on the south-eastern edge of the Shingles Bank, approximately 60 yards north of the south-west Shingle Buoy, which is just over a mile west of the Needles Lighthouse.

The barge lies north-east and south-west and is slowly being covered in shingle. Not much to interest the wreck diver here, but a good hideout for crabs and lobsters. Being on the southern edge of the Shingles, a nasty sea can be kicked up, even in fairly light conditions, so care needs to be taken when diving here.

Yarmouth 6 miles; Lymington 7 miles.

10 Caroline Susan. At 50 40 24; 01 40 40. Depth: 15m. This British motor yacht foundered at this position. The 23 ton boat sank on June 13, 1940. Another report suggests that she may have hit a mine as there was an explosion. Diving information needed.

Yarmouth 7 miles; Lymington 8 miles.

11 Unknown. At 50 38 24; 01 40 24. Depth 21m. A wreck or obstruction was located in this position during a survey in 1981. Little information was gained other than that it stood 1.8m high. This is very little to go on, but it should be worth locating and diving this one to ascertain whether this is a natural feature or a new wreck.

Yarmouth 8 miles; Lymington 9.5 miles.

12 Serrana. Bows of. At 50 39 37; 01 36 06. Depth: 12m. Though she was torpedoed on January 22, 1918, ten miles west of St. Catherine's Point, the *Serrana* struggled hard to reach port. Oberleutnant Stöter in *UB-35* hit her with one torpedo, killing five men, but the 3677 ton British steamer stayed afloat long enough to reach the Needles Channel. The next day at seven minutes past three in the afternoon, her voyage from London to Barbados came to an abrupt end. As she started sinking, she grounded on the Needles Bridge, and just half-a-mile from the Needles Lighthouse she broke her back.

Her stern section quickly broke away leaving her bow and holds firmly embedded where she struck. The stern section drifted away before sinking to form another wreck site only half-a-mile to the north-east. (See Site 6).

The *Serrana,* which was operated by Scrutton and Sons, had been built by J. Readhead and Sons in 1905. She was 353ft long with a beam of 48ft and her 399hp engines gave her a top speed of 11 knots. She was carrying a general cargo.

The bow section broke up swiftly under the pulverising effect of fierce tides and the heavy seas which build up on the Needles Bridge, and is now mostly a large pile of steel plates and girders. Among the wreckage can be found a large amount of her cargo – bricks, railway lines and wagon wheels are scattered around. A few bits of the wreck stand up to a maximum height of three to five metres and there is a lot of fishing tackle to be found draped around them for this is a very popular site for local boats taking out angling parties.

The bottom here is of rock and sand. Divers should plan dives on the bow section carefully. Tides are exceptionally strong.

Yarmouth 5 miles; Lymington 6.5 miles.

13 Millmer. At 50 39 30; 01 34 00. Depth: 6m. The shores of the Isle of Wight and Hampshire are littered with the wrecks of yachts. This is one of them. The *Millmer* burnt out and sank on September 23, 1981 one mile east of the Needles Lighthouse and close inshore under the high cliffs. She is now very broken.

Yarmouth 6 miles; Lymington 8 miles.

14 Kylin. At 50 40 00; 01 36 00. Depth: 6m. The British Ballerina Class sloop *Kylin,* 21 feet long, sank on September 25, 1977, after hitting some submerged object off the Needles. Position is not definite and diving information is not available.

Yarmouth 4 miles; Lymington 6 miles.

15 HMS Assurance. At 50 39 42; 01 35 27. Depth: 11m. One of the Isle of Wight's historic and protected wrecks. No diving is allowed within 75m of the above position. The *Assurance* was protected on April 11, 1974. Discovered by Isle of Wight diver Derek Williams she had struck the same rock as *HMS Pomone* (see below) though many years earlier.

HMS Assurance, a fifth-rate of 44 guns, captained by Carr Scrope, was homeward bound from Jamaica when she ran on to Goose Rock off Needle Point just after dawn on April 24, 1753. Unlike the *Pomone,* the 133ft long *Assurance* did not ride right over the rock, but perched upon it for several hours enabling the crew and the passengers – they included Governor Trelawney of Jamaica and his lady – to get ashore by boats before *Assurance* finally sank. The *Assurance,* the fourth to bear the name in Navy records, was built at the Heather Yard, Bursledon, and launched on September 29, 1747.

At the court-martial, held aboard *HMS Tyger* in Portsmouth Harbour on May 11, 1753, Captain Scrope was acquitted, but the Master David

British fifth rate Pomone of 38 guns, sunk in 1811, after striking a rock just south of Needles Point (Site 15).

Patterson was sentenced to three months in the Marshalsea Prison in London under the 26th Article for running the ship upon the rock. Marshalsea Prison used to stand opposite Maypole Alley in Borough High Street, Southwark, London, and was an Admiralty jail and the county jail for felons and debtors. It was the prison made famous by Charles Dickens in *Little Dorrit.*

The wreck site consists of cannon and other artifacts, such as copper nails, sounding leads, clay pipes, and some coins.

HMS Pomone. At 50 39 42; 01 35 27. Depth: 12m. This British fifth rate of 38 guns was 150ft long and of 1076 tons. She sank on October 14, 1811, when coming through the Needles Passage in the dark and striking a rock about 400 yards to the south-west of Needles Point. She went right over the rock and started to fill with water. The wind then pushed her on to Needle Point itself. Captain R. Barrie ordered the masts cut away and she stayed afloat long enough for her crew of 284 to escape without loss. Many of her guns were salvaged. As a result of this wreck, the Admiralty ordered that Naval ships should not come through the Needle Passage at night.

Some cannon and artifacts from the Pomone were found just south of Needle Rock by teams working on the protected wreck of *HMS Assurance* (see above.)

Yarmouth 5 miles; Lymington 6 miles.

Dream. At 50 39 42; 01 35 27. Depth 11m. No diving on this schooner for her remains lie entangled with those of the protected wreck site of *HMS Assurance* (see above). The *Dream* of 162 tons was built at Yarmouth in 1837-38 and her bell clearly marked and dated "1838" has been recovered on the site of the protected wreck. Presumably she too hit that rock off the Needles and sank down on top of *Assurance* and *Pomone*. It is possible that a Roman ship hit the rock too because 17 Roman coins have been found on the site.

16 Campen. This wreck is 30 yards south of the Middle Needle. Depth: 10m. But you can't dive her without permission of the owners, the Needles Underwater Archaeology Group. Though she is not all that far from the Needles protected site (See Site No 15) the Campen is a much earlier loss.

Her story starts when a small fleet of Dutch East Indiamen sailed from Texel on October 12, 1627. There were seven ships together – the *Prince William, Nassau, Wieringen, Vliegende Draeck, Vlielandt, Terschellingh,* and *Campen*. All were bound for the East Indies and they carried cargoes for the settlements out there – and gold and silver to buy cargoes for the return voyage. This autumn fleet was soon in trouble in the Channel, fighting a south-westerly gale, which seemed to increase more with every hour. Despite this, four ships clung together. Soon it was clear that they were losing ground to the gale and were being driven perilously close to the Needles – so close in fact that they took the amazing course of "trying to thread the Needle" and sail in between the jagged peaks into the calm of the Solent.

Even in flat calm it is something that small boats do with great care. The fact that the Dutch ships tried it tells a great deal about the state they were in. The four ships were the *Vliegende Draeck,* the *Prince William,* the *Terschellingh,* and the *Campen*. First to go through were the *Prince William* and the *Terschellingh* and amazingly enough they went through clean as a whistle. The *Vliegende Draeck* was next and was nothing like so lucky. She struck a rock in the gap and ripped her bottom open. Even so she lurched through and foundered not far up the Solent. The *Campen* was the last to try. She too struck a shallow rock in the centre of the gap, stopped dead, swung round beam on to the wind and almost at once started to break up. There were about 160 aboard, but they all reached shore on makeshift rafts.

Some salvage was done on the Dutch ships almost immediately and large quantities of coin was raised – but not all of it by any means. In the days of modern diving equipment practically every name in the business had a look for the *Campen,* but though we now know that many finned within a few feet of the wreck, it was left to Northampton BS-AC to find it by accident in June 1979. They found piles of lead ballast ingots first, then cannonball, and then silver coin. These were either Spanish-American pieces of eight or Dutch "lion dahlers", a rare coin minted for only a few years at the turn of the 16th century. In all the diving team have recovered some 8,000 coins, and many items of intense interest to historians, such as lidded brass shot containers to hold a made-up charge of gunpowder and a cannonball all ready for firing – though the containers were known it was not thought before this that they were used at such an early date.

All the coin now seems to have been recovered, but the site is still watched over by the Coastguard on the cliffs just above the Needles and the keepers in the Needles Lighthouse, so keep clear.

Yarmouth 5 miles; Lymington 6 miles.

The iron-hulled Irex, *wrecked in Scratchel's bay on her maiden voyage in 1889. Courtesy Blackgang Chine Museum.*

17 Irex. At 50 39 33; 01 34 57. Depth: 6m. The *Irex*, a fully-rigged iron-hulled sailing ship of 2347 tons, was 302ft long. On December 10, 1889, she left the Clyde on her maiden voyage to Rio de Janeiro, Brazil, with a cargo of pig iron, earthenware pipes and pots. She was commanded by Captain Hutton, and carried a crew of 32.

The voyage was plagued with bad weather, and it was not until New Year's Day, 1890, that she was able to stand away from the sight of land. The south-west gales soon returned and were to last more than three weeks. On January 23, after taking a battering which left her crew sick and exhausted, the weather cleared sufficiently to enable her position to be fixed as in the Bay of Biscay. With many of his crew sick and injured, and the cargo in need of restowing, Captain Hutton turned the ship to run back to the English coast. Hutton was exhausted; he had not been able to go to bed for 24 days. On reaching the South Coast he sailed aimlessly along looking for a haven from the storms. As he approached the Needles, the

The compass from the ill-fated Irex.

flashing red warning light from the lighthouse was mistaken for that of a pilot boat. The *Irex* turned toward the light, and only at the last minute did Captain Hutton realise his mistake. It was too late and his ship grounded, heavily smashing open her hull.

A massive rescue operation was mounted and 29 men were finally rescued by breeches buoy from the high cliffs. The ship was doomed and, although a large amount of salvage work was carried out, the weather soon broke the ship up.

Today the rusting hull and the remains of her cargo can be found on the bottom of Scratchell's Bay. The site is just 200 yards off the beach, close west of St Anthony's Rock.

Yarmouth 4.5 miles; Lymington 6 miles.

18 Varvassi. At 50 39 40; 01 35 31. Depth 10m. This Greek steamer of 3874 tons was bound from Bona, Algeria, for Southampton with a cargo of 7000 tons of iron ore, 300 tons of tangerines, many large tubs of wine, and some cattle which she took on at Algiers. After unloading part of her cargo at Southampton she was to go on to Boulogne.

At 10 a.m. on January 5, 1947, in a bad storm the Greek ship, which was built in 1915, was entering the Needles Channel when something went wrong and she ran aground on the Needles Bridge, just 100 yards from the lighthouse. A huge swell was running and it was clear that the *Varvassi* was

in dire need of assistance. But when the Yarmouth lifeboat arrived together with a tug, she was told she was not needed and so returned to Yarmouth Harbour. Meanwhile the salvage officer who had boarded the ship from the tug found her hard aground and water in all her holds. The salvage officer was concerned about the safety of the crew and asked the lifeboat to return.

In huge seas and with the wind rising the Yarmouth boat was called again at 5 p.m. She stood by for four hours before she was told once again that she was not needed. At 6.30 a.m. the next day the lifeboat was called out yet again. This time it was third time lucky and despite the fact that seas were breaking right over the steamer, the lifeboat managed to draw alongside. She had to do this time and time again as the ropes between them broke, but in the end the crew of 35, the salvage officer and a pilot were safely taken off.

It was clear then that the *Varvassi* was doomed and soon her back was completely broken. The stern section, from some 36ft aft of the funnel slid off the rocks and sank. The bow section remained firmly jammed on the rocks, but finally that could not be seen at High Water. Over the years parts of the wreck reappeared at Low Water and several small boats were lost by hitting parts of it. Despite the damage to her very early on, the cattle were all saved and so were 35 tons of tangerines, though the wine seems to have floated ashore and been lost!

Divers will find that some parts of the wreck still lie only a few metres below the surface on a seabed of rock and sand. Most of the wreckage is well broken and scattered with some parts almost 100 yards away from the actual site of the wrecking. The most recognisable parts are the two large boilers at the centre of this rummage dive. Strong tides mean that great care must be taken to take advantage of slack water.

Yarmouth 5 miles; Lymington 6.5 miles.

19 Teamwork. At 50 39 41; 01 35 34. Depth: 4m. This British fishing vessel sank on February 13, 1983 just 200 yards from the Needles Lighthouse. She is now very broken.

Yarmouth 5 miles; Lymington 6 miles.

20 Unknown. At 50 39 50; 01 35 35. Depth: 14m. A very small obstruction was located in this position, a quarter mile to the north-west of the Needles Lighthouse in 1965. It may be a small cabin cruiser. Diving information not available.

Yarmouth 4.5 miles; Lymington 6 miles.

21 Unknown. At 50 38 17; 01 34 11. Depth: 25m. An obstruction was noted in this position in 1982. Local fishermen say it is an outcrop of rocks. No diving information is available to confirm this, so it will be worth a dive to find out for sure. It certainly appears to be of a good height, standing 3-4 metres off the mainly sand and shingle seabed, 1.5 miles south-east of the Needles.

Yarmouth 6 miles; Lymington 7 miles.

22 Albion II. At 50 36 37; 01 34 44. Depth 30m. "Reindeer" is what local fishermen call her, but a bell recovered from this site, though badly worn, indicates that this is really the *Albion II*, an Admiralty trawler of 240 tons, which sank after hitting a mine off St. Catherine's Point on January 13, 1916.

She was found by a salvage firm in June, 1975 and though upright and complete, is now breaking up. She lies east-west, and is about 160ft long.

The remains stand five metres proud of the gravel and sand seabed.
Yarmouth 8 miles; Lymington 9 miles.

23 Borgny. At 50 36 28; 01 36 20. Depth: 33m. This Norwegian steamer
was carrying a cargo of coal from Newport for Rouen, when she was
torpedoed on February 26, 1918 off the Needles. All the crew were saved,
but there is a bit of a mystery about this sinking – no U-boat commander
claimed responsibility and the detail of the sinking was taken into Lloyds
wartime casualty lists from a report in a Kristiania (Oslo) paper of the time.

The 1149-ton *Borgny* lies east-west, is badly broken and is 3m proud of
the seabed. The ship was 229ft long with a beam of 36ft.

Yarmouth 8 miles; Lymington 9 miles.

24 Azemmour. At 50 32 00; 01 36 00. Depth: 25m. The position of this 897
ton French steamer is not confirmed. The position given here is only
approximate. It is certain though that she was torpedoed by Kapitanleutnant Fritz Wassner from *UB-59* on the surface in the morning dark of
March 20, 1918. It was on this cruise from March 10 to March 28 that
Wassner accounted for the *Tweed* (Site 214), the *Venezuela,* and the *South
Western* (Site 217).

The *Azemmour* was 205 feet long with a beam of 33.
Yarmouth 13 miles; Lymington 14 miles.

15 Coquetdale. At 50 30 02; 01 40 21. Depth: 36m. This British steamer of
1597 tons was part of a small convoy running from St. Helen's Road for
Plymouth, though that was not to be her final destination. She was travelling
in ballast from Portsmouth bound for the Clyde and is described as being
"OHMS", which merely means that she was now under Government control
as was much of British shipping in the early stages of World War Two.

The *Coquetdale* was unfortunate in that she became involved on the very
first day of a new phase of the Battle of Britain on August 8, 1940. The
Luftwaffe needed to destroy more R.A.F. planes to put Fighter Command
out of action. To draw up the fighters they launched major bombing attacks
on convoys in the Channel using some 400 aircraft. The aircraft they used
for these attacks on shipping were the slow Stuka dive bombers from
Generalmajor Wolfram von Richthofen's 8th Fliegercorps stationed at Caen.
These "decoy ducks" – even the Germans called them that – were meant to
provide such a tempting target to the Spitfires and Hurricanes that they
would be drawn into positions where clouds of escorting Messerschmitts
could fall upon them.

The Spits and Hurricanes came all right, but the result was not quite what
was expected. The Stukas proved to be a costly liability and from August 8
to 18, a day on which one German squadron alone lost 16 Stukas, they were
so decimated that they were withdrawn from the Battle of Britain altogether.

Not that the decision to do so came in time to save the convoy in which
Coquetdale sailed and which was 15 miles west of St. Catherine's Point
when the Stukas fell down on them from the clear skies of the afternoon of
August 8. The screaming siren of the Stuka was intended to strike panic into
those beneath it. This was no gimmick.

That siren had so unsettled troops in Poland and during the German
conquest of France, that it had almost overshadowed the real power of
these dive-bombers. In the right pilots' hands they were a highly accurate
means of pin-point bombing. In the case of the *Coquetdale*, this was only

The Coquetdale, *victim of a Stuka attack in 1940, first bombed and then strafed by machine gunfire. Courtesy John Clarkson.*

too true. The first bomb struck her amidships and then the wing guns and those of the Stuka observer strafed her from end to end. Within moments the *Coquetdale* was sinking and the 23 men of her crew only just had time to get away in the boats before she sank completely from sight.

The *Coquetdale* was 245ft long with a beam of 37ft. She now lies with her bow to the west and is very broken on the sand-shingle seabed. She stands five metres proud at her highest point.

Yarmouth 15 miles; Lymington 16 miles.

26 Ajax. At 50 30 02; 01 40 21. Depth: 36m. This 942 ton Dutch ship was in the same convoy heading for Plymouth as the *Coquetdale* when they were dive-bombed on August 8, 1940 (see previous site). The *Ajax* suffered more. She was hit several times by bombs, killing four of her crew of 19 and one Navy gunner. She sank within minutes of the *Coquetdale* and her wreckage is almost entangled with that of the British ship. The *Ajax* is six metres proud of the seabed, but there is no scour around her, probably because she is so broken and sinking deep into the sand-shingle bed. She lies south-east to north-west and is just behind the *Coquetdale*.

Yarmouth 15 miles; Lymington 16 miles.

27 Unknown. At 50 28 54; 01 38 24. Depth: 35m. A wreck standing five metres proud of the seabed of stones. Found only by echo-sounder. Diving information required.

Yarmouth 14 miles; Lymington 15 miles.

28 Terlings. At 50 28 15; 01 33 37. Depth: 37m. This 2318 ton British steamer had not long left Southampton heading, in ballast, for Sydney, Australia, when she was caught by German bombers on July 21, 1940. She did her best with her single gun, but was hit and sank swiftly. Of her crew of 27 with one gunner, ten were lost.

The *Terlings* was 283ft long with a beam of 44ft. She now stands eight metres proud of the sand and shingle seabed. She is well broken.

Yarmouth 17 miles; Lymington 18 miles.

29 Unknown Obstruction. At 50 41 25; 01 35 55. Depth: 8m. An obstruction was located in this position during 1981. It is quite small and stands a maximum of one metre off the seabed. This position is 2 miles north-west of the Needles on the western side of the Shingle Bank. No other information is available.

Yarmouth 4 miles; Lymington 6 miles.

30 Beverley Ann. At 50 42 00; 01 33 18. Depth: 20m. This 32ft fishing boat sank near the north-east Shingles Buoy on November 19, 1969. Very broken and is often covered by shingle.

Yarmouth 2 miles; Lymington 3 miles.

Area information and services

Admiralty Charts: 2045 (Outer Approaches to the Solent); 2219 (Western Approaches to the Solent).
Ordnance Survey: 195; 196.
Local weather: (0898) 500403. Marinecall (0898) 500457. For Mid-channel forecast. Southampton Weather Centre. Southampton (0703) 28844.
Weather area: Wight.
Local Coastguard: 999 (emergencies). At sea VHF Channel 16. Solent Coastguard, Lee-on-Solent (0705) 552100.
Local BS-AC Branches: Basingstoke Branch No. 609 hold their dry meetings at the Forrest Ring Community Centre, Winklebury, Basingstoke on Tuesdays from 9.30 to 11.00p.m. Wet meetings are held at Westfield Lido on Tuesdays, 8.30 to 9.30p.m. The branch welcomes visiting divers who can contact Tim Chissel. Tel: (0256) 471726. The branch own a Zodiac and an RIB.

New Forest and Waterside Branch, No. 591, hold dry meetings on the first Monday in the month at the Cross Keys, Totton and wet meetings at La Sainte Union College, The Avenue, Southampton, on Wednesdays from 8.00 to 9.00p.m. The branch own a Chinook IV.
Accommodation: From the Dorset border to the coast of Southampton Water, Lyndhurst Tourist Information Centre, Main Car Park, Lyndhurst, Hants, will supply lists of accommodation of all kinds. Tel: Lyndhurst (042128) 2269. On the Isle of Wight, the Isle of Wight Tourist Office, Quay Store, Town Quay, Newport, Isle of Wight PO30 2EF, will supply holiday information and accommodation details throughout the Island. Tel: Isle of Wight (0983) 524343.
Air supplies: Southern Sea Services, 18 Beaulieu Road, Christchurch. Tel: Christchurch (0202) 48594. To 6,000 psi. Pumping any time by appointment. Diving equipment, test and service. Open: 9.00a.m. to 5.30p.m. weekdays.
Outboard services: West Solent Boat Builders, The Boatyard, Keyhaven. Tel: Lymington (0590) 42080. Running repairs to all makes. Larger inboard engines catered for. Crane available.
Boats for hire: From Poole or Swanage. Nat West (skipper-diver Frank Elston) 12 divers. 33ft, all electronic gear. (0202) 884077. From Poole, *Buccaneer* (skipper Jim Scott) 6 divers; 24ft; all electronic gear; midweek and weekend (0202) 732894.

Area 2: Lymington to The Hamble; Totland to Egypt Point

This area runs from 01 33 00 to 01 18 00 and takes in most of the Western Solent, Southampton Water and the Hamble. The north-west coast of the Isle of Wight from the end of Alum Bay to Egypt Point close to West Cowes is also covered.

Once more great care must be taken with the tides. Tidal streams in the western Solent are very strong with the east-going flood reaching nearly three knots and the west-going ebb even stronger with three-and-a-half knots often recorded. In the main channels the diver-cox'n will find that the streams turn at almost the same times.

Off Yarmouth Harbour the last of the flood tide eddies west towards Sconce Point where it turns out to rejoin the east-going flood. In the same area, to the north of Black Rock, which dries and lies 800 yards west of Yarmouth Pier, a patch of very disturbed water can often be seen. This is known as Fiddlers' Race and is believed to be named after a ship lost here with a band of musicians on board. The area should be avoided by small boats, particularly in bad weather.

Yarmouth has two High Waters. After the first one, the tide falls a little for about half-an-hour then rises again into the second High Water. It then ebbs to the west until Low Water. Slack water periods occur at about one-and-a-half hours before High Water Portsmouth and four-and-a-half hours after High Water Portsmouth. They usually last for 15-30 minutes only, but are sometimes a little longer at Low Water slack.

There is little diving of interest from the northern side of the Solent, much of the land being marshy and the water very shallow, with poor visibility, but the Isle of Wight side does offer more interesting sites.

In fact, in the Totland and Yarmouth area interested crowds tend to gather when divers appear. This makes a change from the mainland where the sight of divers is now so commonplace that no one gives them more than a passing glance!

N.B. Divers should note that much of this area falls under the jurisdiction of the Port of Southampton. In fact the eastern limit of Southampton Port is out in the Solent bounded by a line drawn joining Old Castle Point, East Cowes, at 50 46 00; 01 16 00, with a point on the mainland 100 yards south-east of Hillhead Beacon. To the west the Port is bounded by a line from Stansore Point at 50 47 00; 01 20 00 to Egypt Point on the Isle of Wight.

Those wishing to dive inside the Port of Southampton's limits should ask the Dock and Harbourmaster's permission. Harbourmaster is Captain M.J. Ridge. Tel: Southampton (0703) 330022.

There is one wreck worth including in this section though it is hardly diveable in its present position. In fact no diving is allowed as the ship is

45

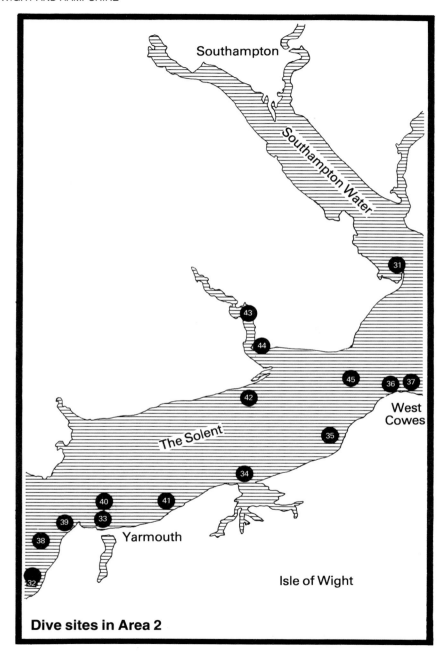

Dive sites in Area 2

protected under the Protection of Wrecks Act of 1973. She is the *Grace Dieu*.

The designation order gives the area within which no interference must take place as within 75 metres of the Ordnance Survey grid reference 501105. Here, three quarters of a mile above Bursledon Bridge in the River Hamble lie some of the timbers of Henry V's great clinker-built battleship. The *Grace Dieu* was built in 1418 and was huge for her time, being only a little smaller than Nelson's *Victory*. She was laid up in the Hamble but was accidentally burnt in 1439. Some of Southampton BS-AC carried out an archaeological diving search of the stern in 1967 in appalling muddy conditions, but not surprisingly found nothing except the ancient woodwork.

Launch sites (Hampshire)

Lymington. Easily reached by leaving the M-27 at Junction One and taking the A337 to Lyndhurst, Brockenhurst and then Lymington, a straight run through the New Forest. Follow the signs for Town Quay. This launching site

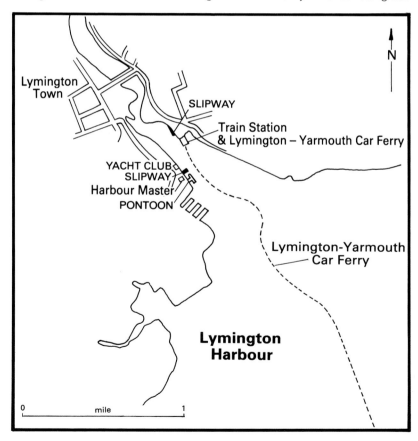

is right beside a small car park in the centre of the town where a concrete slipway gives access at all states of the tide. There is a chain across the slip, but this is easily removeable by means of a twist shackle. There is no charge. Speed limit in the river is six knots.

Diver cox'ns must take great care in this area. Lymington is an important yachting centre with marinas providing hundreds of berths for boats. In addition to these hazards, the Sealink car and passenger ferry runs from here to Yarmouth and all craft must give way to them.

The Lymington River exits through mudbanks into the Solent two-and-a-half miles north-east of Hurst Point. The whole of the River and the shipping activity around Lymington is controlled by the Harbourmaster, Captain F. Woodford, who can be found at the Harbour Office, Bath Road, Lymington close to the Royal Lymington Yacht Club. Tel: Lymington (0590) 72014 and 77262. There is another slipway close to the Harbour Office, concrete onto shingle, useable at all states except at extreme Low Water Springs. Parking is nearby. No anchoring is allowed within the approach channel or the harbour area.

There is no diving without the Harbourmaster's permission and this will not be given except in cases of emergency. High Water at Lymington is minus 55 minutes on Springs and plus 5 minutes on Neaps on the Portsmouth tables.

Buckler's Hard. This launch site is unlikely to appeal to divers wishing to launch inflatables and small boats as it is some distance from the sea and is very, very "yotty". The launch of a powerboat could cost nearly £30 for a day launch and retrieve and is entirely at the Harbourmaster's discretion. There is ample parking for car and trailer nearby. Approach is made by a private road from the road from Beaulieu. The river is under the total control of Lord Montagu of Beaulieu. Speed limit is five knots. Harbourmaster is Mr. W. Grindey. Tel: Buckler's Hard (059063) 200 and 234.

Lepe. At the Country Park on road from Exbury to Calshot is a large car park with toilets. Easy launch over a low groyne, but a long pull over mud at low tide. Restaurant with teas and snacks at back of beach.

Calshot Spit. Approach by B3053. From Calshot follow signs for Calshot Activities Centre. Proceed along road flanked by beach huts to huge hangars of the old R.A.F. flying boat base. It has another claim to fame – it was once the home of the R.A.F.'s High Speed Flight which won the Schneider Trophy in 1931 and flew and developed the prototype of the Spitfire in time for the Battle of Britain.

The Calshot launching slips are magnificent – designed for flying boats not inflatables! – and are right under the eyes of the Coastguard tower and Calshot Castle. One of the slips, of ashphalt, launches inwards towards Fawley the other, of conrete, into Southampton water towards Warsash. There is vast parking space at the Centre. Slips can be used at all states of the tide. Toilets and showers available. There is a charge. Tides are strong. Slack is one hour after High Water Portsmouth. Launching is controlled by Calshot Activities Centre. Tel: Southampton (0703) 892077 or 891380.

Fawley. Shortly after leaving the A326 for the B3053 turn left for Ashlett. In the village turn left at hardware shop on corner and follow sign for Ashlett Hard. The launch site, which is hard shingle, is right beside the Jolly Sailor pub. Ashlett Harbourmaster's telephone number is Fawley (0703) 894184 or 894343. There is a launch charge for the slip which is useable for three hours either side of High Water. Parking available close by.

Marchwood. A public hard at end of Husbands Shipyard but very rough, with a mixture of shingle and mud with a tiny parking place above it. Beware of a group of rocks some 100 feet from the edge of the slip. These show at Low but catch props on exit at other times.

Eling Wharf. Off the A35, follow signs for Eling Village. Site is close to the Anchor Inn pub, but is shingle and steep. There is a nasty drop off at the end. Available three hours either side of High Water. Very muddy exit into creek.

Southampton (St. Denys). From the city centre follow signs for St. Denys Station, then for Priory Hard to south of rail station. Actual launch site is in Priory Road. Available at most states of tide, this concrete slipway is free. There is parking nearby. Launch is into River Itchen. The speed limit is six knots.

Southampton (Weston). This site is off the A3025. Follow signs for Weston. Go down Weston Parade and the site is on Weston Shore. Available at most states of the tide, there is no charge and parking is nearby. Launch is into Southampton Water.

Netley. Follow signs from A3052 for Netley Abbey. Launch site is in Beach Lane which is approached from Victoria Road. This is a concrete slipway, but is only useable for two hours before and after High Water. There is no charge. Slip leads down to shingle.

Hamble River. There are many launch sites for small boats here and they are well used. The sites give access first to the River Hamble and so into Southampton Water and from there into the Solent. There is a speed limit in the river of six knots.

The river counts as a harbour and has a Harbourmaster, Captain C.J. Nicholl, O.B.E., whose office is in Shore Road, Warsash. Tel: Locks Heath (04895) 6387. The river is navigable at all states of the tide and High Water is the same as Portsmouth. No anchoring is allowed within the approach channel or harbour, which is just as well as the river is packed solid with moorings as far as Bursledon Bridge and even further up than that. There are four major marinas too. There is, of course, no diving without the permission of the harbourmaster.

Launching sites are numerous. Here are just three of them, which the diver will find particularly useful:

Lands End Public Hard, Bursledon. Turn off A27 at Bursledon. Look for Moody's Boatyard and Jolly Sailor pub. Here the shingle foreshore is useable at all states of the tide. Park at the station a quarter of a mile away. No charge.

Warsash Public Hard. Leave A27 and follow signs for Warsash. Shingle hard is close to the Rising Sun pub. Car parking nearby. Use at all states of the tide. No charge.

Hamble Quay. Concrete slip is close to the Bugle Inn pub at the end of the High Street and right next to the Royal Southern Yacht Club. Parking is close but fills early. No charge. It is useable four hours either side of High Water.

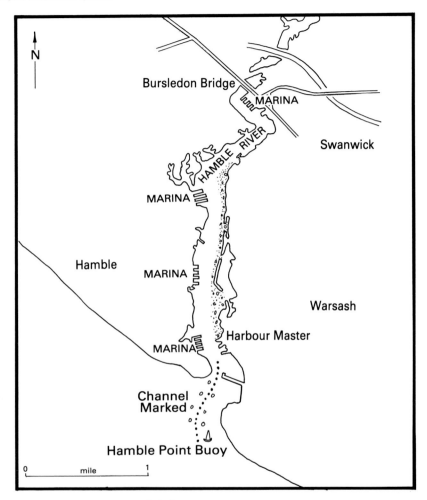

Launch sites (Isle of Wight)

Colwell Bay. Small concrete ramp leads on to sandy beach. It is privately owned and there is a charge. Good parking close by. Located at end of Colwell Chine Road, off A3054.

Yarmouth. There are two concrete slipways into the harbour and one wooden slip into the River Yar. Winch available. All are useable at all states of the tide. Car parking is nearby. Speed limit is six knots in the harbour and the river. Slips are free.

Gurnard. There are two little shingle beaches in Gurnard Bay. A stream runs across the westerly one. The other is backed by a concrete promenade. The sailing club is here and the concrete slip is close by, but there is little parking close to the slip which is useable for three hours either side of High Water, and is free.

Egypt Point. This slip is at the junction of Egypt Hill and the Esplanade of West Cowes. Made of concrete, the slip is useable for three hours either side of High Water. Parking close by. Launching free.

Shore dives (Hampshire)
These are few and far between on the Hampshire shore in this section. Best is at Calshot Castle.

31 Calshot Castle. Diving here is from the Calshot Activities Centre, who must be phoned in advance and told of numbers of divers coming. (See launch site detail). If asked to do so they will then clear the diving with the authorities. The area falls well inside the eastern limit of the Port of Southampton (see Introduction to this section) and all diving must be notified and permission obtained. Even so any shore diving here must have boat cover, unless the divers are roped. The viz is usually poor and the area is used by local clubs for novice training. Depths close offshore are down to 12 metres. Close in though, to the east of the Castle there is "The Hole". Here depths go down from five metres to 18m and there are said to be large congers. Tides are strong and eddies make the search for slack difficult. Official slack is one hour after High Water Portsmouth or one and a half hours after High Water Southampton.

Flying Boat. At 50 49 16;01 18 24. Depth 10m. This is the final resting place of a flying boat which was found by the Southampton Harbour Board during a survey of the area in 1971. The site is just 700 feet to the north of Calshot Spit Point. The aircraft was dived by the Navy, who reported the plane upside down and almost buried in the mud. It appeared almost intact apart from the tail section which was missing altogether. Latest reports suggest that the aircraft is now very broken.

Shore dives (Isle of Wight)

32 Totland Bay. Lies between Hatherwood Point and Warden Point and is one-and-a-half miles long. A pier, with a depth of two metres at full Low, sticks out from the coast about 600 yards south of Warden Point.

Cream jars recovered from beneath Totland Pier.

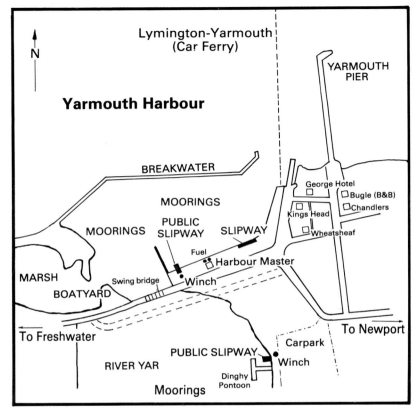

It is the pier which seems to act as the centre of all the diving activity and this is a favourite dive site for local divers. Parking at Totland is not usually a problem, but a charge for it is made in the summer months.

Entry to the water is easy from the beach or from the head of the pier. The seabed is mainly sandy and flat with a maximum depth of seven metres at High Water. Just to the south of the head of the pier is an area which has produced some fine old bottles. This may well have been a dumping area, for the dates of the bottles vary too much for any one shipwreck.

Tinker Shoal, a rocky ledge with a depth to the top of about two metres, runs out some 800 yards to the west of the pier. Marine life is small, but visibility in the area can be very good.

33 Yarmouth. This is a popular harbour with a pier at its entrance. The pier, about 200 yards long, has a depth of three metres at its head at low tide and is used by Solent cruise boats and anglers. Some shore diving is done here but with caution as strong tides run through the area and the large Sealink car ferries from Lymington pass very close to the pier every half hour. The seabed is mostly mud with a covering of sand and shingle. Maximum depth is about eight metres at High.

N.B. There is no diving without permission of the Harbourmaster, Captain G. Holland, whose office is on New Quay. Tel: Yarmouth (0983) 760300. High Water in the harbour is at minus one hour on Springs and plus five minutes on Neaps on the Portsmouth tables. Anchoring in the approach or harbour is not allowed.

34 Newtown. This small village is halfway between Yarmouth and Cowes on the north-western shore of the Island and the area is dominated by the estuary of the Newtown River with its 14 miles of narrow creeks and marshland. This and the adjacent four miles of the Solent shore are owned by the National Trust and form an 800-acre nature reserve. Newtown, a thriving port in the 17th century, was once the capital of the Island. It is now very popular with yachtsmen during the season.

The lakes formed by the river are shallow and muddy, but can be dived if permission is granted by the Harbourmaster. Tel: Calbourne (0983) 78424. Landing at Fishhouse Point at the entrance to the estuary is banned during the nesting season for seabirds, April to June. On the Solent shore only shallow dives are possible. To the west of the harbour entrance the beach is shingle and runs steeply to the seabed. To the east it is mainly sand and the seabed is generally flat.

The main problem here for divers is access. There are no roads around the fingers of the estuary or to the shore, so diving means a long hike with gear along pathways.

35 Thorness Bay. Access to the beach here is possible only through the Haven Holiday Centre. A road runs through the Centre down to the mainly sandy beach. Permission to use it should be obtained from the centre office. Diving is shallow, but can be interesting around the various rocky outcrops.

36 Egypt Point. The most northerly point of the Isle of Wight. It is midway between the harbour at Cowes and the village of Gurnard. Access to the water here is easy with plenty of good car parking spaces on the main road which runs along the top of the beach. You can walk from the car down the steepish shingle beach and straight into the water.

Once in the sea the steady downward slope continues with the shingle giving way to an area of weed at 8-10m. Within this weedy area is a small bank running parallel to the shore.

Pattons' Hotel (formerly the Holmwood) showing the slipway (Site 36).

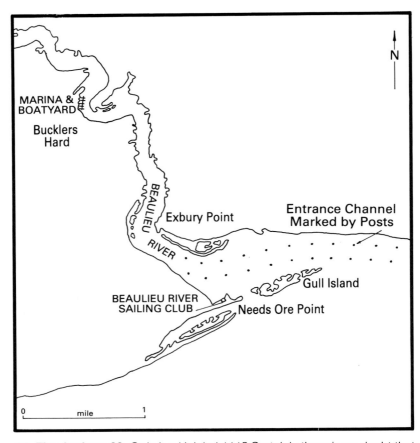

MARINA & BOATYARD

Bucklers Hard

BEAULIEU RIVER

Exbury Point

Entrance Channel Marked by Posts

Gull Island

BEAULIEU RIVER SAILING CLUB

Needs Ore Point

N

0   mile   1

37 The Junkers 88. Or is it a Heinkel 111? Certainly there is no doubt that on the bank in the area of weed at Egypt Point are the remains of a German bomber shot down during World War Two after bombing Portsmouth. Pieces of aluminium sticking out of the weed give away the crash site. This is an interesting area with the weed hiding many parts of the plane. One engine was recovered some years ago, but the other engine has yet to be found. Some of the items which have been found – a machine gun, one of the propellor blades and local artist's picture of the crash are in the possession of the previous owner of Paltons Hotel.

Divers should be warned that though they are very close inshore here, the tide does run hard and it is easy to underestimate its effect. Slack water in the area is one and a half hours before and four hours after High Water Portsmouth and the longer slack is on the Low Water period.

Boat diving sites:

38 Toccatina. At 50 42 12; 01 33 00. Depth: 5m. This British yacht was

sunk on August 10, 1977 in this position just off Hurst Point, West Solent.
Yarmouth 2 miles; Lymington 3 miles.

39 Jo-Anne. At 50 42 30; 01 31 00. Depth 9m. This 26-foot-long fishing
boat sank off Fort Victoria, Yarmouth, on July 16, 1976 following a collision
with a buoy. The Jo-Anne capsized, but all her crew were saved.
Yarmouth ¾ mile; Lymington 2½ miles.

40 Yarmouth Roads Wreck. At 50 42 52; 01 29 59. Depth: 7m. Here lies
another historic and protected wreck. This one is of a 16th century
shipwreck, so far unidentified, but which may be the 600 ton Spanish *Santa
Lucia*, wrecked in 1567 while carrying wool to Flanders. A bronze saker gun
made in Venice has been found as well as pewter and some ship's timbers.
Excavation has started. Diving, apart from that being done under the
guidance of archaeologists, is banned within 50m of the above position.
Yarmouth ½ mile; Lymington 3 miles.

41 Margaret Smith. At 50 42 54; 01 28 08. Depth: 16m. The *Margaret
Smith* is a modern wreck, a 300 ton gravel dredger, measuring 141′ × 21′
× 8′. She can be found just a mile to the east of Yarmouth Harbour.
On June 28, 1978, she was approaching Cowes Harbour when a series of
rough seas made her to roll hard several times. This caused her cargo of
gravel to shift and she listed heavily to starboard. Her master was soon
unable to control her. A "Mayday" call was sent out, and within a few
minutes a rescue helicopter was on the scene. A crewman was lowered on
to the listing ship and he told the crew to put on their lifejackets and to board
their liferaft. Just as the last man entered the raft, *Margaret Smith* started to
roll over. The helicopter crewman ran across the side of the ship to pull the
liferaft clear. Later all the crew were safely winched up into the helicopter.
The *Margaret Smith* was now completely upside down but still afloat, and
starting to drift on the ebb tide down the Western Solent. The local tug
Calshot, was able to secure a line to her and towed her to just outside
Yarmouth, where she was secured to one of the Admiralty moorings. Shortly
afterwards she sank.
Today the wreck is intact, and lies on her starboard side with her bows to
the west. Her port side is only 8m below the surface. There are several
portholes still there but they are well fixed. Her hold is now empty and only a

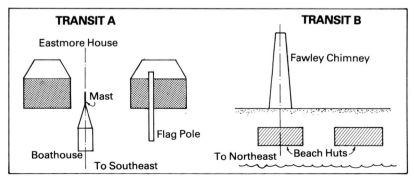

Marks for the Margaret Smith (Site 41).

few small piles of gravel remain. Her small box wheelhouse still has its radar scanner in place. Behind the wheelhouse the door to the engine room hangs open, a home now for conger eels. For many years her five-foot-diameter bronze prop was still in place.

The site is fairly well protected from the prevailing winds, and is a good dive when the weather elsewhere is not so good. Beware the strong tidal streams.

Yarmouth 1 mile; Lymington 3 miles.

42 Landing Craft. At 50 45 46; 01 25 48. Depth: 5m. This wreck is a small landing craft upside down in shallow water approximately 1½ miles west of Needs Ore Point, near the Beaulieu River. It was found by Island diver Dougie Saunders when helping a local fisherman to recover some fishing gear. He says "It was a landing craft upside down in the mud. The fishing nets were caught around the drive shafts and props. The bottom was wooden and fairly rotten. I meant to go back and have another look, but I never quite got round to it".

Yarmouth 4 miles; Lymington 3.5 miles.

43 Minca. At 50 48 16; 01 25 03. Depth: 2m. Known as the old Minca Barge, this wood with metal fittings barge was abandoned by the Army after World War Two after it broke free from its moorings and stranded here up river. Not so much a dive as a mud-bath!

Yarmouth 7½ miles; Lymington 7 miles.

44 Wooden Landing Craft. At 50 47 52; 01 24 28. Depth: 2m. Hardly a serious dive, but a wreck all the same. This small wooden landing craft was abandoned by the Army at the end of WW2 and parts dry.

Yarmouth 7 miles; Lymington 6½ miles.

45 Algerian. At 50 46 00; 01 20 19. Depth 24m. This British steamer of 3837 tons was built of steel in 1896 by the Sunderland Shipbuilding Company. She was 364ft long with a beam of 45. She was bound for Southampton in ballast when she hit a mine in the Western Solent on January 12, 1916. At the time of her loss she was owned by the Ellerman Line and all her crew were saved.

She sank in the middle of the deep water channel just a mile west of Egypt Point. Due to the danger of other ships hitting her, she was dispersed many times, the first being in 1920. Later most of her superstructure was blown off though she is still six metres proud in places. Most of her is well-broken and her plates lie flat on the seabed, probably pushed that way by the extremely strong tides which sweep over the site and have also created a one-metre scour around her. The wreckage lies north-east to south-west and she is little dived, mainly because of her position in the centre of a busy shipping channel. Great care is needed diving here.

Yarmouth and Lymington 7 miles.

Area information and services

Admiralty Charts: 2045 (Outer Approaches to the Solent). 2040 (The Solent – Western part and Yarmouth Harbour).1905 (Southampton Water and Approaches). 2219 Western Approaches to the Solent.

Ordnance Survey: 196.

Local Weather: (0898) 500403. Marinecall (0898) 500457. For mid-channel forecast. Southampton Weather Centre. Southampton (0703) 28844.

Local coastguard: 999 (emergencies). At sea VHF Channel 16. Solent Coastguard. Lee-on-Solent (0705) 552100.

Local BS-AC Branches: Romsey Branch No 1259 holds its wet meetings at Stanbridge Earl School, Romsey from 7.30p.m., followed by dry meetings at the Duke's Head from 9.00p.m. Visiting divers welcome. Contact Ian Smith (0794) 523944. The branch owns two inflatables.

St Edward's Sub Aqua Club, BS-AC Branch No 1675, hold wet meetings on Thursdays 8.00-9.00p.m. at St Edward's School, Nelchet Court, Shirfield English, Romsey, followed by dry meetings. The branch owns an RIB. Contact: Brian Overton (0794) 523339.

Diving Services: Scuba Techniques, Elmsworth Lane, Porchfield, Isle of Wight. Tel: (0983) 529023. Dive instruction courses.

For other services see Area One.

Area 3: Warsash to Stokes Bay; Cowes to Ryde

This third area runs from 01 18 00 to 01 10 00 and covers a large section of the Eastern Solent, which is without question one of the busiest waterways in the world. Diving must be undertaken only with great caution. Much of the diving here will come under the jurisdiction of the Dockyard Port of Portsmouth whose western limit begins exactly where the eastern limit of the Port of Southampton ends (See Area Two).

Once again this is an area dominated by the tides. In the Central and Eastern Solent those streams are very strong. In Cowes Roads, for example, they reach 3-4 knots. In Cowes Harbour and the River Medina the tide floods for six-and-a-half hours and ebbs for almost five hours. The ebb is particularly strong in the narrows where a floating bridge operates between East and West Cowes. Here it reaches 5-6 knots and many small craft are unable to enter the river until the stream has slacked off. The run is strongest on the eastern side.

On Spring tides, after the first High Water, the tide falls a little and then rises again to make a second High Water about an hour later. After this the tide ebbs away to the west until Low Water. On Neap tides only one High Water occurs. Slack water comes around one and a half hours before High Water and 4-5 hours after High Water Portsmouth and lasts between 15 and 30 minutes.

In the area of the Calshot Light Vessel, the tidal streams tend to be rotary. The last two hours of the ebb stream divide here and run east and west past the Bramble Bank. Captain John Coote, R.N. in his revision of the "Shell Pilot to the South Coast Harbours" (Faber and Faber) draws particular attention to the dangers of the Bramble Bank.

He advises yachtsmen: "Whether coming from east or west remember the Bramble Bank, situated in mid-Solent. In spite of being such a well-known danger, yachts still go aground on this shingle shoal which may vary from year to year in depth and position. At lowest Springs it used to be the scene of an annual cricket match organised by Uffa Fox." There is at least one wreck on the edge of the bank today (See Site 49).

All the tides in Southampton Water are tricky. On Springs there are two High Waters. The young flood rises for about two hours after Low Water. It then becomes fairly slack rising only slowly for another two hours. Then the

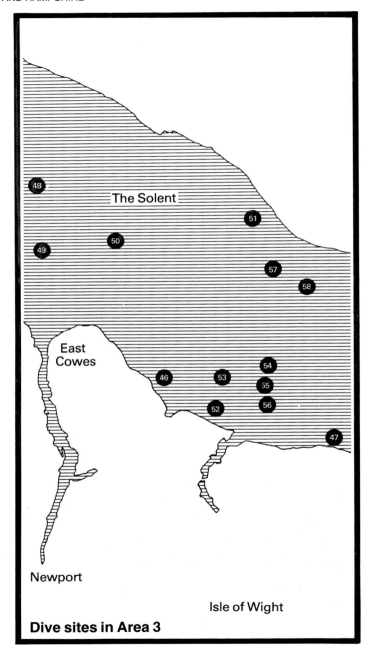

The Solent

East Cowes

Newport

Isle of Wight

Dive sites in Area 3

main flood sets in for almost three hours until High Water is reached. After this the tide level drops a few inches for about an hour and then rises again for about one-and-a-quarter hours until a second High is reached. The second High is about the same height as the first. This long stand of High Water was one of the reasons that Southampton became a major port as it allows deep draught ships to manoeuvre for long periods.

On Neaps the High Water stays for a long time with no appreciable drop in level. In fact, within Southampton Water, there is little drop in level as long as the west-going stream is running through the Solent, but when the Solent stream turns to the east the water rushes out at high speed for about three and a quarter hours. The most rapid fall is during the two hours after the second High Water on Springs. Within Southampton Water slack water occurs at approximately High Water and there is little movement for up to two hours. A much shorter slack occurs at about five hours after High Water Portsmouth.

In the eastern part of the area – between East Cowes and Ryde and Hill Head and Stokes Bay on the Hampshire coast – the streams follow the direction of the Solent. Their strength varies considerably with up to two knots on the east-going and two-and-a-half knots on the westward run. The further east one goes the slacker they get. Slack water is about two hours before and four hours after High Water Portsmouth and lasts 15-30 minutes.

Warning: As a result of a number of incidents during which small boats hampered the movement of really big ships in the main channel near Calshot Spit, Southampton's Dock and Harbourmaster has issued the following tough Notice to Mariners:

"Yatchsmen, mariners and owner/skippers of small recreational craft are advised of a new requirement when navigating in the vicinity of the main navigable channel in the Calshot Spit area.

"In view of the increasing movement of large deep-draught commercial vessels, which are severely restricted in their ability to manoeuvre while rounding the Calshot Turn, and the difficulties experienced with yachts and other small craft passing through the main channel, it has been found necessary to introduce a restriction in the following area – 'That part of the main navigable channel defined on Admiralty charts Nos. 1905, 394 and 2040, which lies between a line drawn from Bourne Gap buoy to North Thorn buoy, and a line drawn from Castle Point buoy to the Reach buoy'.

"The transit and movement of yachts and all small craft through this area is NOT PERMITTED AT ANY TIME. Failure to comply with this direction may lead to prosecution."

Dive boat skippers should obviously take careful note.

Launch sites (Hampshire):

Lee-on-Solent. Take B3385 to seafront and Marine Parade East. A concrete slipway is useable for 4 hours either side of High Water. No charge. Parking close by.

Stokes Bay. Take B3333, turn off to seafront. Three concrete slipways are available at various points. Useable four hours each side of High Water or alternatively a launch over shingle is possible at all times. No charge. Parking nearby.

N.B. There is a 10-knot speed limit within half-a-mile of the shore.

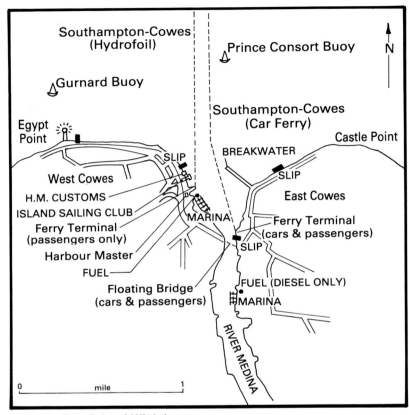

Launch sites (Isle of Wight):
Cowes. Famous as the leading yacht racing centre of the world, Cowes houses the headquarters of the Royal Yacht Squadron. It possesses the most convenvenient harbour for the Solent and is protected except from winds from the north and north-east. Keeping order out of chaos during Cowes Week and during the rest of the year too is Harbourmaster Captain H.N.J. Wrigley, who can be found at his office on the Town Quay. Tel: Cowes (0983) 293952. There is a speed limit of six knots in the harbour and the River Medina and no anchoring in the approach channel or the harbour. Needless to say there is no diving in the harbour without Captain Wrigley's permission. Diver cox'n should take great care when navigating in this area – car ferries, passenger ferries and hydrofoils can make life very exciting – not to mention the yachts when racing! High Water in the harbour is minus 15 minutes on Springs and plus 15 minutes on Neaps on the Portsmouth tables.

Launch sites:
West Cowes Esplanade. Concrete slipway available for three hours either side of High Water. No charge. Parking nearby.

Dover Road, East Cowes. Site is next to the Red Funnel Terminal, off Trinity Road. Three hours either side of High Water. Concrete. No charge. Parking nearby.

Fishbourne. Large ramp at Sealink Ferry Terminal, Fishbourne Lane, off A3054. Check if all right to use at Sealink Office.

Quay Road, Ryde. Ryde has many slips. This one is of stone to beach near the Hovercraft terminus and is useable for three hours either side of High Water. No charge. Parking nearby.

Shore diving (Hampshire):
There is little shore diving of any value on this section of the Hampshire coast, but some divers do go off the shore in search of flatties.

Shore diving Sites (Isle of Wight):
46 Osborne Bay. Offers some very shallow diving from the shore, but conditions are generally very murky. Shore divers here should be careful to keep right in as further out the tide run is very fierce.

47 Ryde. Few places can have so many piers as the Isle of Wight. In the Victorian hey-day of the pier, the Island boasted no less than nine – one for every six-and-a-half miles of coastline! Today there are only six of those piers left. Ryde Pier is the largest of them and is the second longest in Great Britain, reaching out to sea for almost half-a-mile. It carries both trains and vehicles to the pier head, where the high-speed Sealink catamarans from Portsmouth decant up to 450 passengers a time. The pier is the base of the

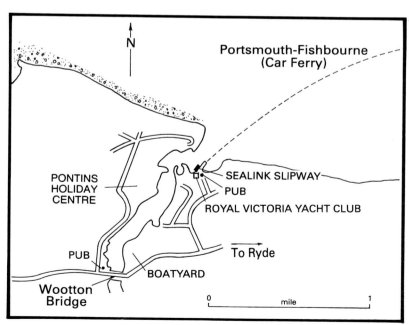

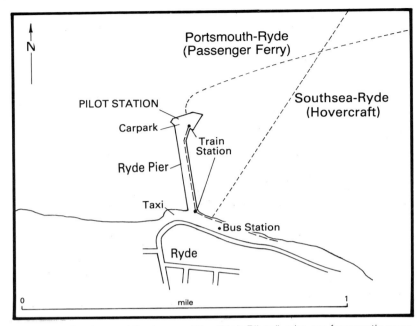

N

Portsmouth-Ryde
(Passenger Ferry)

Southsea-Ryde
(Hovercraft)

PILOT STATION

Carpark

Train
Station

Ryde Pier

Taxi

•Bus Station

Ryde

0   mile   1

Ryde Pilot Station and the home of the "Nab Pilots", who are frequently seen being ferried out towards the Nab Tower to board inbound ships. During the summer months the pier is also busy with the Solent cruise boats.

The pier had to be long to reach the deep water at the edge of the wide expanse of Ryde Sands. The diving straight off the beach is not very exciting – it would be more rewarding down from the pier at low water! The business end of the pier is a different matter. The pier head covers a very large area and interesting diving can be had in and around the pier supports. The depth is 10m at High Water. The seabed is a mix of sand, mud and many years of interesting items which have fallen from the pockets of those above or – in the case of the engagement rings found by divers – thrown in by disappointed or betrayed maidens! Entry and exit points here are few and not always available. Ask for permission to use them before diving.

Boat diving sites:

48 Luciston. At 50 47 57; 01 18 03. Depth: 18m. Oberleutnant E. Steindorff on his mission out of Zeebrugge in UB-74 on December 22, 1917, was no respecter of Christmas – or perhaps he just slavishly followed his orders to patrol the English Channel and to sink any Allied ships he encountered. Certainly his log shows that he was near the Owers Lightship on his way west on Christmas Eve. Hull down in the dark just before Christmas Day he spotted the 2877-ton British steamer *Luciston*. He fired one torpedo which hit her full in the port side. Despite this the *Luciston* struggled on making for Southampton, but finally had to be beached near the mouth of Southampton Water, 1¼ miles from Calshot Point.

There she stuck fast, despite all attempts at repairs. In 1922 they blew away a portion from her stern to her boiler room, but the rest of the wreckage remained with 10m of water over her bow at Low and 18m at her stern. Dispersal attempts went on for years with the last recorded in 1963. As a result she is well broken and lies on the side of a bank. This is a favourite angling site and abandoned anchors are plentiful!

Oberleutnant Steindorff lasted until May 26, 1918 when he was caught off Portland Bill in *UB-74*. There were no survivors from the U-boat when she was attacked by the anti-submarine yacht *Lorna*. After two depth-charges were dropped four objects bobbed up in the midst of the foam. Another depth charge went down and the explosion blew the four objects into the air. They were German sailors. That explosion killed three of them. Only one was still able to cry 'Kamerad' when picked up by the shocked crew of the *Lorna,* but he died from his injuries within three hours.

Bembridge 10.5 miles; Portsmouth 8 miles.

49 Chain Ferry. At 50 47 45; 01 17 30. Depth: 10m. An old Chain Ferry which used to operate on the river Medina between east and west Cowes, sank in this position while being towed from Cowes to Southampton on February 3, 1976. The position is close to the Bramble Bank about half a mile south of the Calshot Spit Light Vessel. She is very broken and very muddy.

Yarmouth 9.5 miles; Lymington 9.5 miles.

50 Florence Vivian. At 50 47 38; 01 16 16. Depth: 3m. There is very little left to see of this fishing vessel sunk in October, 1923 on the East Knoll. Divers report the odd small piece of wreckage.

Bembridge 10 miles; Portsmouth 7 miles.

51 The Bumps. At 50 47 40; 01 12 30. Depth: 1-3m. This area is charted as "Foul Ground", but apart from the very bumpy seabed there seems no reason to call it "foul" and divers have found it a good area for big flatfish.

Bembridge 8 miles; Portsmouth 5 miles.

52 Peel Wreck. At 50 44 52; 01 13 22. Depth: 5m. This site, known as the Peel Bank Wreck, is, in fact, a large concrete structure and located one mile to the north-west of Wootton Creek. It is fairly small – around 4.5 metres square and is often referred to as a concrete barge. It is more likely that this is a section of Mulberry Harbour. Many of these units were anchored in this area prior to being towed across the Channel to France during the Normandy landings in June 1944. At Low there is only a few feet of water over the site and on calm days the tide can be seen bubbling around it. The seabed is mainly mud and shingle. The site is marked by a large red buoy marked PEEL WRECK, which is to the north-east of the site.

Bembridge 6 miles; Portsmouth 5 miles.

53 Unknown. At 50 45 22; 01 12 43. Depth: 4m. This is a very small obstruction lying on the edge of a mud bank half-a-mile to the east of the Peel Bank Buoy. It stands about 1.5 metres high and there is a scour around it of less than half a metre. It may be a small boat of some kind. There is no other information on this one, but it is in very shallow water and would be a fairly simple, snorkel dive to find out.

Bembridge 6.5 miles; Portsmouth 4.5 miles.

54 Unifloat. At 50 45 33; 01 12 01. Depth: 18m.

55 Unifloat. At 50 45 32; 01 11 46. Depth: 18m.

These two are marked on Admiralty charts as separate obstructions alongside one another.

The first is the larger section which is the obstruction to the west. It is approximately 100ft x 30ft in size and lies north and south. It is mainly steel plates and ribs sticking out of the muddy bottom with a maximum height of 2m and is the remains of several Unifloat pontoons. Around the site are many bits of rope, wire, plates and bottles.

The second is the smaller section to the east. This section lies north and south and is made up of five Unifloat-type pontoons. Length in all is 65ft with a beam of 30ft. The pontoons stand three metres high and were part of the D-Day operations.

The whole site lies on the side of a mud bank on the southern edge of the shipping channel and is 1½ miles north of the entrance to Wootton Creek. The area is well protected from south-westerly winds and makes a good dive when the weather is not too good.

Bembridge 6 miles; Portsmouth 4 miles.

56 Ibis. At 50 45 45; 01 11 36. Depth: 16m. The British fishing vessel of this name was 26ft long and sank on April 25, 1984. The position given is that of her sinking, but local experts believe that the wreck may have moved a little with the tides from that point. Diving information required.

Bembridge is 6 miles; Portsmouth 6 miles.

57 R.T.C. No. 9. At 50 46 37; 01 10 54 (Bow). At 50 46 36; 01 10 39 (Stern). Depth: 16m. *R.T.C. No. 9* was an old steam-powered, steel hopper barge. At one time she was owned by the River Tyne Commisioners (RTC).

On August 3, 1893, she was in collision with *H.M.S. Endymion,* half-a-mile off Stokes Bay beach. The 317-ton barge was cut in two and sank. She measured 102ft x 28ft x 12ft.

The two sections of barge sank about 100 yards apart. The larger section is the bow, about 65ft long and it lies in an east-west direction, standing almost 4m high. Most of the wooden decking is missing and the hold is well silted.

The stern section is around 30ft long and stands 3m high. Within the wreckage can be seen the remains of her small steam engine. There is a deep scour around this section of some 2-3m in the seabed of mud and sand. The wreck was definately identified in 1972 when a diver recovered her bell which had the inscription "SCREW HOPPER No. 9".

For many years this wreck was known as the *Weston Maid*. The site is marked by a green wreck buoy.

Bembridge 5.5 miles; Portsmouth 3 miles.

58 Tank Landing Craft 1068. At 50 46 43; 01 10 31. Depth: 10m. This Mark IV LCT was badly damaged by gunfire during ship target trials on June 4, 1947. Two days later, while being towed across Stokes Bay by a salvage vessel, she sank just half-a-mile off Stokes Bay Beach. All type IV LCT's were of 586 tons and measured 187ft by 39ft with a draught of five feet. They were powered by twin Davy Paxman diesels and fitted with two 20mm. guns.

The remains of this one can be found about 25 yards inside the wreck buoy and is broken into three parts on the sand-mud and shingle seabed. The highest point of the wreckage is 3m. proud, but much of it is buried in

The 90ft Newclose takes parties of 12 to 30 divers, and offers complete live-aboard facilities.

the seabed. The parts which show are covered with deadmen's fingers and anemones and there appears to be a resident shoal of pouting. This is a simple dive with an inflatable launch from one of the Stokes Bay slipways. Make sure of diving on slack – about two hours before High Water Portsmouth or four hours after. The wreckage lies in a north-west and south-east direction.

Bembridge 6 miles; Portsmouth 3 miles.

Area Information and services

Admiralty Charts: 2045 (Outer Approaches to the Solent); 394 (The Solent – Eastern part); 1905 (Southampton Water and Approaches); 2793 (Cowes Harbour and River Medina).

Ordnance Survey: 196.

Local Weather: (0898) 500403. Marinecall (0898) 500457. For mid-channel forecast. Southampton Weather Centre. Southampton (0703) 28844.

Local coastguard: 999 (emergencies). At sea VHF Channel 16. Solent Coastguard. Lee-on-Solent (0705) 552100.

Local BS-AC Branches: Wight Dolphins No. 807 are a very friendly and helpful bunch of divers. Wet meetings are held at West Wight Pool, Freshwater on Fridays from 7.45 to 10.00p.m. Visiting divers are welcome. Visitors who wish to join the branch on their dives should contact the Diving Officer Brian Paddock (0983) 296505.

Accommodation: Lists and details from Southampton Tourist Information Centre, Above Bar Precinct, Above Bar, Southampton. Tel: Southampton (0703) 221106. Isle of Wight accommodation details from Isle of Wight Tourist Office, Quay Store, Town Quay, Newport, Isle of Wight. Tel: Isle of Wight (0983) 524343.

Air Supplies: Andark Diving and Watersports, 256, Bridge Road, Lower Swanwick, Southampton. Tel: Locks Heath (04895) 81755. To 4,000 psi. Owned by professional diver Andy Goddard, Andark is a fully-stocked dive shop and also provides servicing and testing of equipment. Diving instruction is available. Open: Mon to Fri. 9.30a.m. to 5.30p.m. Sats: 9.00a.m. to 5.30p.m. Suns: 10.00a.m. to 4p.m.

Southern Cylinder Services, Gallery 18, Fort Fareham Industrial Estate, Fareham. Tel: Fareham (0329) 221125. Owned by Peter Judge, this is a service workshop for test and service of diving equipment, and supplies air to 4,500 psi. Open: 8.30a.m. to 5p.m. Mon to Fri. Sats: 8.30a.m. to 12 noon.

Swift Marine, 2-4 William Street, Southampton. Tel: Southampton (0703) 229485. commercial and sport diving shop. Also test and servicing. Air to 3,000 psi. Open: 8.30a.m. to 5p.m. Mon to Friday.

Sub-Aqua Products, 63-65 Twyford Road, Eastleigh, Hants. Tel: Eastleigh (0703) 612144. Fully stocked retail dive shop. Test and service. Repairs to suits, wet and dry. Air to 3,400 psi. Open: Tues to Sat 9a.m. to 1p.m. 2p.m. to 5.30p.m. Closed Suns and Mons.

Air Supplies (Isle of Wight): Diving and Marine Services (I.O.W.), 75 Staplers Road, Newport, Isle of Wight PO30 2DG. Tel: (0983) 525169. Run by Martin Pritchard, is a BS-AC School. Air to 230 bar, equipment supplied and serviced. Will advise on dive sites.

Boats for hire: At Newport *Newclose* (Skipper John Gallop). Minimum 12 divers, maximum 30. 90ft, electronic gear. Parties picked up at Southampton Round island cruising and diving. From Island Charters, 48, Quay Street, Newport. Tel: Isle of Wight (0983) 525728.

Constable, based Hamble, can pick up at Portsmouth (skipper John Skilton); 8 divers; 30ft; electronic gear. Tel: (0489) 786174.

Strenuous, based Southampton, but will pick up at Portsmouth or Lymington (skipper Des Pearce); 12 divers per day or 8 live-aboard; 50ft; electronic gear. Tel: (0703) 550143.

Area 4: Gosport to Hayling Island; Ryde to Culver Cliff

This section runs from 01 10 00 east to 00 56 00 and the end of Hampshire. It extends south to 50 40 00. This means that it takes in a great deal of exciting diving and includes the Nab Tower, the Solent Forts, and a mass of highly diveable wrecks.

Once again the diver intent on exploring this section must take strong tides into full account particularly when wreck diving.

At Spithead and to the west of Spithead the west-going stream runs for about 5 hours, which is between 2½ hours before and 2½ hours after High Water Portsmouth. The east-going tide runs for 7 hours with no appreciable slack at the end of the run. In the outer approaches to Portsmouth the first four hours of the flood tide is fairly slow with the last three hours rising faster. The ebb stream runs for five hours, starting slowly but picking up quickly once the east-going tide stream picks up at Spithead. The later part of the ebb is the strongest, reaching 4½ knots on Springs between the 3rd and 4th hour.

At the entrance to Portsmouth Harbour the first 4 hours of flood runs across the channel towards Langstone Harbour, then for one hour it makes towards Southsea Castle, then turning directly into the Harbour entrance. The ebb first sets to the west, then south-west, then finally south-east running between 2½ and 3 knots for 3 hours.

Within Portsmouth Harbour the flood tide runs in two periods reaching speeds between 1-3½ knots. The ebb runs in one period reaching 5 knots through the narrows. The strength of both streams drops quickly further inside the Harbour. There are frequently eddies on either side of the harbour entrance. A small boat channel is on the western side of the entrance and small craft should use this both going in and out of harbour. The only true slack water off the entrance occurs at 1 hour after High Water Portsmouth.

In both Langstone and Chichester Harbour entrances the tidal streams are very strong, reaching up to 6 knots on Spring tides. Off the entrance the west-going stream starts at around 2 hours before High Water and the east-going one around 3 hours after High Water Portsmouth.

In the southern part of this area, to the east of Bembridge, the flood tide runs south-east through the Solent and north-east around the Isle of Wight shoreline. Both flood and ebb are strongest running along the eastern side of the Island, reaching 2.4 knots on the flood and 2.7 knots on the ebb. Slack water occurs at around 1 hour before and 5 hours after High Water Portsmouth. Inshore the ebb can start around 2 hours before High Water Portsmouth.

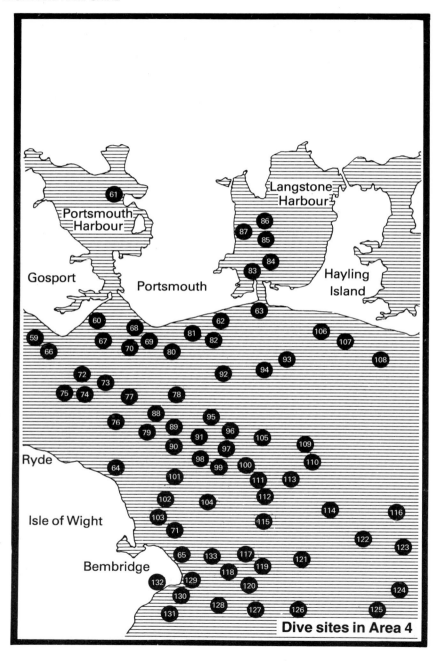

Dive sites in Area 4

Launch sites (Hampshire):

Gosport Hardway. Close to Hardway Sailing Club and Priory Road, this is a concrete slipway available for five hours either side of High Water. Use is free. Parking nearby for car and trailer.

Portsmouth. The great Naval port, known as "Pompey" to countless sailors. The entrance to the port is very, very busy and diver cox'ns must take great care in this area. There is a speed limit of ten knots inside the

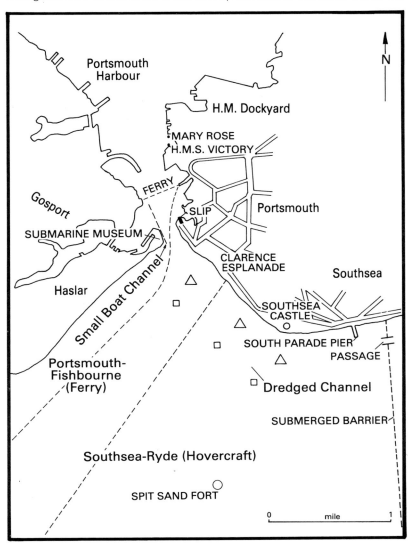

harbour, which is ruled by the Queen's Harbourmaster, Captain C.J.T. Chamberlen from his office in the Dockyard. Tel: Portsmouth (0705) 822351 Ext. 23124. No diving is permitted in the harbour or within 150m of any R.N. ship. The Dockyard Port of Portsmouth's limits to the east stretch from near Hayling Island right down to Sandown Bay, Isle of Wight, but the Harbourmaster does not enforce the no-diving-without-permission rule further than the actual harbour limits.

Camber Quay, East Street. This is an old ferry slip, is the best small boat launch site in Portsmouth and is wide and made of concrete. Launching is possible at all states of the tide, but note the slip barrier can be locked after five p.m. on weekdays, and at weekends. There is special ample parking for car and trailer, though customers of the nearby Bridge Tavern seem to think they can park there too! Charge for boats up to 5m is £1; over 5m £2. Best plan if you intend to use this slip is to telephone the Berthing Master, Mr.S.G. Grist in advance and sort out the times you wish to use it. Portsmouth (0705) 834764. Mr. Grist is very helpful and warns diver-cox'ns of the danger from the big car ferries which may come in nearby at speed and can send a great surge of water at the slip.

Langstone Harbour. Two launch sites enable divers to explore the sheltered waters of the harbour and the shallow wreck sites.

Eastney. From A2030 follow signs for Hayling Island Ferry. Close to the Eastney Cruising Associaiton Clubhouse is a concrete slip available at all states of the tide. Ample parking for car and trailer. No charge for slip.

Hayling Island. A wide concrete slipway useable free at all states of the tide is near the Ferry Boat Inn and the Harbourmaster's office. Parking nearby.

Launch sites (Isle of Wight):
Seaview. 1) A small concrete ramp on to the shingle beach at the junction of Puckpool Hill and Springvale Road, but note that parking is difficult.
2) Concrete slip on to beach at end of Pier Road. Reasonable parking and a small boat park as well.

St. Helen's. Good ramp on to shingle and sand beach at The Seashore, off Duver Road. Good parking available nearby.

Bembridge. This shallow harbour is protected from westerly and southerly winds. A speed limit of six knots is enforced by Harbourmaster Mr. M.H. Coombes, who can be found at the Harbour Office. Tel: Bembridge (0983) 872828. High Water is the same as Portsmouth. There is no anchoring within the approach channel or harbour and there is no diving without the permission of the Harbourmaster.
Launching is by means of private slips for which there is a charge. Useable for two hours either side of High Water, one of these slips will be found at the premises of Bembridge Outboards, and another at A.A. Coombes Boatyard.

Foreland. A long, narrow and steep ramp onto shingle and rocky beach. At the end of Paddock Drive. Parking only in road and is limited. This one is only really suitable around High Water.

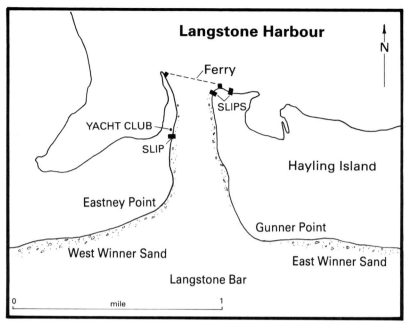

Langstone Harbour

N

Ferry

SLIPS

YACHT CLUB

SLIP

Hayling Island

Eastney Point

Gunner Point

West Winner Sand

East Winner Sand

Langstone Bar

0   mile   1

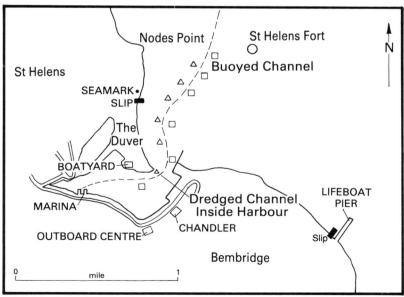

Nodes Point

St Helens Fort

N

St Helens

Buoyed Channel

SEAMARK
SLIP

The
Duver

BOATYARD

Dredged Channel
Inside Harbour

LIFEBOAT
PIER

MARINA

OUTBOARD CENTRE

CHANDLER

Slip

Bembridge

0   mile   1

Shore dives (Hampshire)

59 Stokes Bay Pier. This ruined pier is at the eastern end of the Bay and is in very shallow water with a maximum of 7m at High Water. The area is often used for training. Around the piles of the pier there is plenty of debris for a rummage and there are flatfish on the sand away from the actual pier remains. Entry is from the beach, with a short swim to the pier. Take care: windsurfers and small boats. Use SMB's. If you are unlucky enough to co-incide with an angling competition – go somewhere else!

60 The Glasshouse. Just another name used for H.M. Detention Centre at Haslar, in front of which the dive takes place. There is a car park beside the golf club and close by is an easy entry point via the steps in the sea wall. Take care if you enter elsewhere – that sea wall is steep and slippery. This is really a dive for novices and instructors. Site is shallow down to 5m. Bottom is sand and gravel with a few small rocks. Marine life is scarce.

61 Horsea Island. This man-made salt-water lake with mud bottom inside Portsmouth Harbour has been the setting for some horrific stories of the tough training of Marines and other fighting men. It does, however, also provide an excellent training ground for divers of the sporting variety and is heavily booked by local clubs for that purpose. Depth is 7m. The lake is M.O.D. controlled and fees are payable for its use. Details and permission to use the lake from Lt-Commander R.A. Newton, Officer-in-command Horsea Island, Phoenix, Matapan Road, Portsmouth, PO2 9PQ. Tel: Portsmouth (0705) 822351. Ext. 25187.

62 West Winner. The stretch of coast from the Submarine Barrier near Lumps Fort to the big bank of the West Winner has been the site of many beach dives. Most, it is true, have been made by Southsea spearfishermen in snorkel gear and many have been the catches of flatfish and other species, including bass. The fit spearfisherman can swim out to the site of the wreck of the *Roway,* which has a post alongside it (See Site 82), but the lung diver will find this too much. Most beach diving is done from around the Pier, Clarence Way, and along the blocks. It is shallow, but there are lobsters to be found there.

63 Fravis At 50 47 16; 01 01 37. Depth: 3m. This old dredger is only a few yards offshore and just qualifies as a shore dive. Now only a boiler and small wreckage is left. N.B. She is close to a sewer outfall. Tide through harbour mouth can be very strong.

Shore dives (Isle of Wight)

64 Seaview. Excellent snorkelling and diving can be had in Seagrove Bay. The best of it is to be found at the end of Pier Road. To find it, approach Seaview from the village of Nettlestone, turn into Seaview Lane (B3340) and then turn right into Old Seaview Lane. As you approach the shops, Pier Road is on your right. Go down it until you reach a section of unmade road and continue on. At the bottom is a good-size parking area. Along the shore are the badly-broken remains of the old sea wall, but at the northern end is a good concrete slipway down to the beach. This makes access to the water easy.

To the south you can climb over a short sea wall onto a steep shingle beach which reaches all the way to Horestone Point.

Bembridge Lifeboat Station, well protected from the prevailing south-west winds, is an ideal location for novice divers.

THe seabed is mainly sand and small rocky outcrops. A short way out are some gullies, much weeded, with plenty of sea life. The viz here is usually excellent and the area is well protected from the predominant south-westerlies.

65 Bembridge Lifeboat Station. The lifeboat pier at Bembridge at Lane End Road is a favourite site for local divers. The area is well protected from the predominent south-west winds so there is nearly always calm water close inshore. Visibility is also usually good.

These conditions make this an ideal area for novice dives or training exercises. There is a car park above the beach and a slipway suitable for launching small boats.

The lifeboat pier is around 150 yards long and about 2 yards wide, with the boat shed and slip at the seaward end. The piles of the pier are set into one metre square concrete blocks and the seabed is a mixture of sand and shingle. About half way out the bottom becomes more rocky with many large stones and boulders, most of which seem to be an anchor for the abundant long strands of seaweed that grow here. The strands stretch right up to the surface of the water. This band of weed is around 15-20 yards wide, stretches both north and south of the pier, and is home to many small fish and lobster. At the end of the pier the seabed becomes rocky again and the maximum depth is around 6-7m. Most diving is carried out 1-2 hours before High Water Portsmouth to ensure a reasonable depth of water, although at this time there is usually a slight tide set to the south, which can sometimes be stronger close in by the beach than further out.

N.B. The Bembridge lifeboat – a Tyne class boat – must never be obstructed in any way. There is also an inshore inflatable rescue boat on site.

Boat diving sites:

66 Duddon. At 50 46 42; 01 09 35. Depth: 6m. This wreck is the remains of the old lighter *Duddon* which broke in two during some salvage operations near the end of Stokes Bay Pier in March 1924. The largest part was to be dispersed with explosives by the Navy, but unfortunately the buoy which

Martin Woodward with bottles of Whitbread's beer from HMS Velox (Site 117) and showing his Maritime Musuem.

Bembridge, apart from its harbour, has yet another attraction for divers. Up the hill from the harbour in the centre of the village is the Bembridge Maritime Museum. This is a must for any diver and will have wreck divers drooling against the glass of the crowded displays of wreck recoveries! The museum is the creation of Martin Woodward, a North Sea diver of the early 1970's, but forced to give that up when the bell was dropped by accident with him in it, damaging his spine. He still dives from his own boat around the Island, and knows more about wrecks in the area than anyone. He is without doubt the leading wreck and salvage diver in the area today. Yet he is always willing to help amateur divers with marks and wrecks for them to explore.

An interior view of the Maritime Museum, a must for divers visiting the Bembridge area.

was used to mark the site was lost and they were unable to relocate it. Later attempts to find the wreck were of no avail. The Navy assumed that as the lighter had been empty the remains had probably drifted away on the tide.

It was not until 1981 when a local fisherman reported an obstruction a quarter of a mile offshore saying that he could stand on it as it nearly broke surface that anyone was sure where the *Duddon* had gone. She is very broken on a sand-mud bottom.

Bembridge 5 miles; Portsmouth 2.5 miles.

67 Unknown. At 50 44 31; 01 06 45. Depth: 17m. A very old wreck, as yet unidentified. This is the wreck of a ship of about 130ft long with a beam of 22ft and she lies north to south. She stands two metres proud of the side of a steep mud bank. Local diver Mike Walsh has studied the site and has unearthed many lumps of concretion, pieces of iron and an extremely old iron anchor.

Bembridge 2.5 miles; Portsmouth 3 miles.

68 HMS Boyne. At 50 46 12; 01 05 20. Depth: 10m. The *Boyne,* of 98 guns, was a three-decker commanded by the Honorable George Grey. On May 4, 1795, she was at anchor at Spithead, provisioned and with enough powder and shot for four months at sea. Not all of her 750 crew were aboard, though her Marines were all there, practising musketry. They were drawn up on the poop, firing and reloading by numbers. Somehow a spark from this shooting blew away and landed still alight in the Admiral's cabin. It was shortly before noon and the spark set light to some packages. In five minutes the rigging was ablaze and the fire out of control.

News quickly spread around Portsmouth that a ship was on fire and crowds poured down to the waterside to watch. So great was the excitement that a court-martial aboard one of the other ships in the anchorage was suspended and all but the prisoners, went on deck to watch the blaze. But other ships, closer to the *Boyne,* moved away – they knew just how much ammunition she had aboard.

By 2p.m. she was a complete mass of flames. Every now and then one of her guns would go off from the heat. Then the cables to her anchors burned through and she drifted with the tide towards the harbour. Finally she ran aground off Southsea Castle. The crowds watching now numbered thousands and they obviously had little idea of the danger they were in.

The *Boyne,* like most warships of her time, had one main magazine, lined with felt and situated below the waterline. In addition to this she had small "ready-use" magazines fore and aft. At 5p.m. the fire reached the aft magazine. The magazine may have been small but the explosion was huge. Portsmouth shook and a great cloud of smoke shaped like a palm tree rose thousands of feet in the air. Out of the smoke came a hail of debris – wood, cannon-balls, bits of iron, and unidentifiable pieces of the ship herself. The debris fell into the sea – and the crowd of spectators.

Yet oddly enough, the only casualties on shore were among a flock of sheep grazing on the common. Fourteen died on board, including the Captain's Clerk, ordinary seamen, four women and three children.

The wreck of this 1800-ton ship, nearly 180ft long obstructed the main channel into Portsmouth for many years, so in September, 1838 she was blown up to reduce the danger to navigation.

Today the Boyne Buoy still marks the site of the wreck and on a great mound of shingle just 200 yards to the east of the buoy are various pieces of ironwork and concreted remains, including the odd cannonball. It is possible that quite a large amount of the ship is still intact under the mound.

N.B. Divers should take great care if diving this site not to stray into the main channel!

Bembridge 4 miles; Portsmouth 1.5 miles.

69 Mary Rose. At 50 45 48; 01 06 10. Depth: 10m. Yes, we do know that the old ship is on display in Portsmouth very close to *HMS Victory!* But the ban on diving for 300 metres round this position still stands as there may well be more archaeological treasures buried under the mud. The fact that the stem and the bowcastle have never been recovered and may be there still is sufficient to make this remain an historic wreck site with full protection. Every diver whether or not he or she took part in the diving work on Henry VIII's battleship sunk in 1545 and recovered in 1982, should pay the old ship a visit and see the splendid exhibition of the things which came out of her. It just shows you the sort of thing that can lie buried under Solent mud!

Bembridge 4.5 miles; Portsmouth 1.5 miles.

70 Spit Sand Fort.

71 Saint Helen's Fort. The Solent Forts were constructed during the 1860's to protect the approaches to Portsmouth and the Naval anchorage at Spithead from attack by French warships.

Work on constructing the forts, which were designed by Captain E.H. Steward, began in July, 1861 but was halted during 1862 due to political problems, to be restarted in 1865. The foundations were made of huge stone blocks which were shaped in Stokes Bay and transported to the sites by barges. At the sites screw piles had been sunk into the seabed and topped with staging on which a railway track was mounted, so that a steam crane could lift the blocks from the barges and then move them around the site and deposit them in the correct place on the seabed with assistance from divers. These foundations, an amazing 59 feet thick at the seabed, were finished in 1869. The forts were fully completed by 1880. The larger forts measured 240ft at the seabed and around 200ft at the top.

A French invasion never materialised, but the forts were reactivated during WW1, although they saw no action. During the interwar years they were neglected but again refurbished and re-armed at the beginning of WW2.

St. Helen's Fort stands by the entrance to Bembridge harbour channel.

HMS Royal George, *sunk in an accident at Spithead in 1782, with the calamitous loss of 900 lives. Painting by Schetky in the Tate Gallery.*

The areas between the two main forts and the seashore at Ryde and Southsea were protected by an anti-submarine defence system made up of large concrete blocks with pillars above water, and a boom of large concrete cylinders was stretched between the forts themselves. Many of these are scattered around the seabed today.

The forts did see some action this time – against attacking aircraft. After the war the forts were deactivated. In 1963 they were put up for sale, but it was not until 1982 that Spit Sand was sold. It has now been renovated and opened to the public as a museum. No Mans Land and St Helen's have both been sold. The remaining fort – Horse Sand has been retained by the Ministry of Defence.

As far as diving goes, Spit Sand is a very busy place with many boats running back and forth, so diving is not to be recommended. St Helen's is situated at the entrance of the channel leading into Bembridge Harbour and is also very busy. It is very shallow with many rocks strewn around the base. Maximum depth here is around 5m.

Spit Sand Fort is 1.2 miles from Portsmouth and 4.4 from Bembridge, St. Helen's Fort is 5.2 miles from Portsmouth and three-quarters of a mile from Bembridge.

72 Many obstructions. At 50 46 45; 01 07 18. Depth: 20m. There are an amazing number of these obstructions in the area between the Harrow and Haslar Banks. They are about the same size as oil-drums – they might be that of course – and are believed to be part of the anti-submarine defences of World War One. Most are within a radius of 200 yards of the above position. All are less than one metre high.

Bembridge 5 miles; Portsmouth 1 mile.

73 HMS Royal George. At 50 45 26; 01 06 45. Depth: 22m. Not so much a wreck site as a burial mound. The Royal George was the flagship of Rear-Admiral Kempenfelt. She capsized at Spithead on August 29, 1782 and nearly 900 lives were lost. That huge death-toll included the Admiral and many women and children. The reason for the tragedy seems to have been that as the 100-gun first rate was about to sail with the rest of the British fleet to relieve Gibraltar which was being beseiged by the French, a last-minute repair needed to be made to some fitting which was just underwater. To heel the ship and bring the leaking point above water, they moved her guns from one side to the centre of the ship. At the same time stores for the voyage were being loaded and the ship was crowded with the women and children of the crew aboard saying their fond farewells. Old and rotten, the ancient ship could not take the load on one side – and something snapped. She went over suddenly and swiftly.

Salvage work was carried out over the years, notably by the Deane Brothers in 1836, and then again by the Royal Engineers from 1841 to 1843. She was located again in 1965 by Alexander McKee during his search for the *Mary Rose*. McKee did not expect to find much of the *Royal George* as the Royal Engineers' liberal use of explosives in the course of raising her cannon from the wreck had been well documented. But he did find her burial mound – of shingle standing some two or three metres above the seabed complete with 32-pounder cannonball and pottery from the ship. The area of the wreckage is large, for the *Royal George* was of 2047 tons, 178ft long with a beam of 51ft.

Bembridge 3.5 miles; Portsmouth 2 miles.

74 Barge. At 50 45 04; 01 06 10. Depth: 30m. This wreck, two miles south of Southsea Castle, was found in 1978 and dived. Here are the remains of a barge sitting upright on a mainly mud bottom. She is 100ft long and stands a maximum of 4m proud. The hold appears to be full of iron radiators and they are well silted in.

Bembridge 3 miles; Portsmouth 2.5 miles.

75 Yacht, name unknown. At 50 45 04; 01 06 25. Depth: 30m. This is the intact wreck of a 30ft yacht. She was first dived in 1971 when her mast lay out to the port side. She is now well silted, but lobsters can be clearly seen clustering under her perspex hatch covers!

Bembridge 3 miles; Portsmouth 2.4 miles.

76 Hovercraft. At 50 44 24; 01 05 56. Depth: 26m. The first diver to find this on a drift dive was very puzzled about what he saw before him. He faced a mass of aluminium with some sort of rubber-compound sheeting on the top flapping about in the tide. It was only after other dives on her that he realised that what he was looking at was a small upside-down hovercraft and the rubber material was her skirt. The hovercraft is very broken, blunt in shape and quite small, some 40ft long. Gauges and filters have been recovered from her.

This may be a hovercraft tested to destruction by the Royal Navy. She stands some 3m proud and lies north to south.

Bembridge 2 miles; Portsmouth 3 miles.

77 Unknown. At 50 45 17; 01 05 08. Depth: 13m. This wreck, first located in 1977 three-quarters of a mile north-west of Horse Sand Fort, was not dived on until 1980. The divers reported finding a steel craft totally upside down. Twin shafts and propellers were visible. The hull was very corroded and was around 50-60ft long. She lies in a north-south direction with her bows to the north. The wreck stands a maximum of a metre off the muddy seabed.

A further dive recently failed to locate the wreck which may have been disturbed or covered in mud during dredging operations.

Bembridge 3 miles; Portsmouth 2.5 miles.

78 Horse Sand Fort.

79 No Man's Land Fort. Both these forts have a depth of about eight or

No Man's Land Fort, popular site for training and second dives (Site 79)

nine metres around them at High Water. Both are popular as second dives and for training. The seabed is mud well covered with shell and stones. The crevices in the foundations are home for both crab and lobster. There are a small number of scallops to be found round about.

The forts can be dived at any time, as there is always a large area of slack on the lee sides. SMB's must always be used, as it is easy to move out into the tide run and be swept well away.

Horse Sand Fort is 3 miles from Portsmouth and 3.5 miles from Bembridge. No Man's Land Fort is 3.2 miles from Portsmouth and 3 miles from Bembridge.

80 Pontoon. At 50 45 36; 01 02 13. Depth: 10m. South of the *Roway,* this pontoon is 12ft square. It has big anchors on it and old pipes around it. It is good for lobsters.

Bembridge 5 miles; Portsmouth 3 miles.

81 Pearl. At 50 46 33; 01 03 58. Depth: 3m. The *Pearl* was an old British sailing barge which foundered just to the east of the submarine barrier off Southsea, on March 25, 1922. The site lies just a quarter of a mile off Southsea beach. The barge was quickly battered to pieces in the shallow water and very little of it remains today. Parts of the heavy wooden keel stand a maximum of 0.2 metres off the sand and gravel seabed. The site is sometimes used as a training place for divers.

Bembridge 4 miles; Portsmouth 2 miles.

82 Roway. At 50 46 05; 01 02 12. Depth: 8m. The *Roway* was a small 110-ton British dredger built in 1937. She was 90ft long with a beam of 19ft. She sank after being hit by a freak wave on May 3, 1967, a mile south of Eastney Point on the Horse and Dean Sand.

In 1970 a contract was placed for raising the wreck, but the salvage attempt was unsuccessful. In 1978 the Portsmouth and Medway diving team from *HMS Vernon* carried out demolition of the upper part of the wreck which was very close to the surface, and had been hit by several small boats.

Today the remains of the *Roway* are fairly intact apart from her upper works. The hull is upright and full of sand and shingle. Parts of equipment used during the early salvage attempts can be seen close to the wreck.

The site is easy to find as it is marked by a pile with a spherical topmark. Bembridge 4 miles; Portsmouth 3 miles.

83 The Prison Hulks. In Langstone Harbour. Depth: 12m. These relics of Napoleonic days, though they housed both prisoners-of-war and Navy men who had offended against the code, are now merely lumps of timber. The hulks were moored on both sides of the harbour entrance, one close to Eastney Lake and the other near the site of today's Ferry Boat Inn. Divers who grope around the moorings have recovered a number of stone jars recently.

Bembridge 6 miles; Portsmouth 3 miles.

84 Mulberry Unit and the **Mask.** At 50 47 55; 01 01 25. Depth: 3m. This concrete unit has broken its back and the rate of break-up seems to be accelerating. It is now in two sections. It dries and can be seen from the shore. At the northern end is the wreck of the *Mask*. This 72ft long former dredger was used in her last days as a scrap recovery vessel. Her mast shows at all states of the tide, but she is very broken.

Bembridge 6 miles; Portsmouth 3 miles.

85 Excelsior. At 50 48 01; 01 01 43. Depth: 12m. This small dredger sank at her moorings one night. She is upright and intact though becoming very fragile. She is heavily silted, but can be good for shellfish. She lies north-south with her bows to the north. Her bell was recovered in 1970.

Bembridge 6 miles; Portsmouth 3 miles.

86 Irishman. At 50 48 18; 01 01 20. Depth: 3m. The *Irishman* was a tug towing *Percy,* a dumb barge laden with crane in Langstone Harbour on May 8, 1941, when she ran into an aerial sea mine dropped earlier by a Heinkel 111 into the main channel. The 99ton tug and the crane barge simply disappeared in a huge waterspout and the crew were killed. The remains of both the tug and the barge lie just off Sword Point on the tip of the Sword Sand bank. Part of the wreckage dries 2m at Low Springs and is marked with a beacon. This site was used for many years as a training dive area for Southsea BS-AC. Most prominent underwater feature is a giant wheel which came from the crane. Otherwise only the stern is just recognisable.

Bembridge 6 miles; Portsmouth 3 miles.

87 Withern. At 50 48 06; 01 01 46. Depth 3-5m. This is a bucket dredger and the wreck is marked by a beacon. She is very broken and lies on a sloping mud bank. A silty shallow dive which might be good for trainees to accustom them to low-viz diving!

Bembridge 6 miles; Portsmouth 3 miles.

88 Buoys. At 50 44 30; 01 05 14. Depth 30m. Signs of a wreck in this position, a quarter of a mile to the North-east of No Man's Land Fort were first found during a 1972 survey. Further surveys in 1975, 1978 and 1980 confirmed its existence. The 1980 survey also reported that the wreckage lay north and south and stood 4m off the seabed and had a metre deep scour around it. There was some additional debris about 175 yards to the south-south-west of the wreck.

The site was dived recently but all that was found was a cluster of buoys and chain. So it may be that this is all there is. Or is this just debris from a wreck yet to be dived?

The site lies within the deep water channel and extra care should be taken here.

Bembridge 2.5 miles; Portsmoth 3 miles.

89 Diadem of Bursledon. At 50 44 27; 01 04 09. Depth: 30m. This wreck is probably the remains of the yacht *Diadem of Bursledon,* which sank on September 24, 1970 a quarter mile to the north-west of the Horse Elbow Buoy.

The site was dived and then the divers report finding an old wooden yacht of which 7m of the stern was sticking out of the mud and standing a maximum of 3m off the bottom. The bows appear to be completely buried.

Bembridge 2 miles; Portsmouth 3 miles.

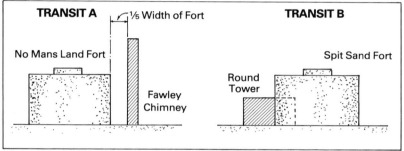

TRANSIT A — 1/6 Width of Fort — **TRANSIT B**

No Mans Land Fort · Fawley Chimney · Round Tower · Spit Sand Fort

Marks for Torpedo Recovery Ship. (Site 90).

90 Torpedo Recovery Ship. At 50 44 10; 01 04 53. Depth: 28m. This wreck, half a mile south-east of No Man's Land Fort, was first located in 1978. It was dived in 1980 and divers reported finding a torpedo recovery ship, the *460A.* She was 65ft long and stands upright on a muddy bed with a maximum height of 4m. Her bows are to the south-east. There is a fair amount of damage to the hull, particularly midships on the starboard side, probably from a collision. The hull is of wooden double-diagonal construction and of a semi-planing design.

Divers can see the tips of the twin propellors by lying on the bottom and looking under the stern. A derrick on the stern has now fallen. The binnacle has been recovered.

Warning: This site lies on the southern edge of the deep water channel leading into Spithead, so diver-cox'ns must keep a sharp lookout for other shipping.

Bembridge 2 miles; Portsmouth 3.5 miles.

91 Cambrian. At 50 44 30; 01 03 22. Depth: 5m. This site lies threequarters of a mile to the south-east of Horse Sand Fort and is the remains of the 388 ton *Cambrian.* This ship was requisitioned for Naval service at the beginning of WW2. She was used as a boom defence vessel, and patrolled the anti-submarine boom defence system which was rigged between Southsea and Ryde, to prevent Axis submarines from getting into the Naval anchorage at Spithead.

The *Cambrian's* active service did not last very long, for she hit a mine and sank eight months later on May 30, 1940. She sank in shallow water and was quite visible, but she was too badly damaged to salvage and as she was well clear of the main shipping channel, she was left to the elements.

Over the years she broke up into several sections and gradually disappeared from sight lying just a few feet below the surface. Because of this some demolition work was carried out in the late 1970's. This has left the wreck well scattered and spread over an area of 280 yards radius around the green conical buoy which marks the site. Very little of the wreck is recognisable. She is mainly a pile of plates and ribs, but is a good shallow dive, worth a rummage.

Bembridge 3 miles; Portsmouth 3.5 miles.

92 Pontoon. At 50 45 44; 01 02 13. Depth 4m. This is an old pontoon lying 1½ miles south of Eastney Point. Any planking that was on it has now disappeared and only the steel framework remains to reveal its function. It is about 10 yards long and 2 yards wide, lying in an east-west direction with a maximum height of a metre off the flat sandy bottom.

Bembridge 4 miles; Portsmouth 3 miles.

93 Margjagulin. At 50 46 22; 01 00 40. Depth: 5m. The 50-foot yacht *Margjagulin* sank in this position, a mile to the south of Gunner Point on the southern tip of the East Winner Sand, on February 5, 1977, after striking a submerged object by the old submarine barrier between Horse Sand Fort and Southsea seafront. The crew were saved. Very little remains as the yacht soon broke in two. The bows were washed ashore and most of the stern was salvaged from the seabed.

Bembridge 5 miles; Portsmouth 4 miles.

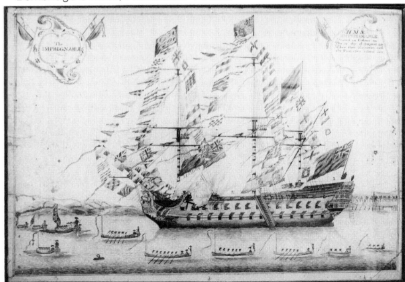

HMS Impregnable *in all her glory. One year later she was a total wreck, though no lives were lost.*

94 HMS Impregnable. At 50 45 53; 00 57 33. Depth: 4m. The 98-gun second-rate man o'war *Impregnable,* Captain Jonathan Faulknor, was 178ft long, 49ft in the beam and drew about 25ft. The 1887-ton ship carried a crew of 190 men, and had been launched at Deptford in 1786. Off St. Catherine's Point in the morning of October 19, 1799, the convoy of 12 merchant ships which *Impregnable* had escorted home from Lisbon without incident, despite the war with France, broke formation and started their run across Sandown Bay ready to turn into St. Helens' Roads for the final leg into Portsmouth.

The wind was blowing strongly from the south and Captain Faulknor handed over charge of the ship to the Master, Michael Jenking. Soon *Impregnable* too was making her home run at a good ten knots. At 6p.m. the cliffs of Dunnose were two miles off. At 6.30 they could see Culver Cliff. It was getting dark now and Captain Faulknor asked Jenking if it would not be better to stand out to sea for the night, but Jenking was determined to get home that night. That was his undoing. Soon the great ship was aground and bumping heavily. Only in the dawn, when they had cut away her masts, could they see that they had in fact bumped a mile-and-a-half right across the Chichester Shoals to near the entrance to Langstone Harbour. The ship was bilged and became a total wreck though everything that could be salvaged was taken out of her. None of the crew were lost. Jenking was dismissed the service at a court-martial though Faulknor was acquitted.

This site is very close to that of *Caduceus* (Site 108). Divers of 308 SAA have found her massive keel, 4ft-long bronze pins weighing 30lbs each, lead piping for bilge pumps, and mounds of cannon balls.

95 HMS Invincible. At 50 44 34; 01 02 23. Depth: 7m. This is a protected wreck site and has been since September 30, 1980 when an order came into effect banning all diving within 100m of her position. She is marked by a spherical yellow buoy lettered "HMS Invincible Wreck".

The story of the discovery of this British 3rd rate 1793-ton 74-gun man o'war starts with Portsmouth fisherman Arthur Mack hand-trawling over the Horse Sands on a May morning in 1979. He snagged and hauled up a massive piece of oak — an old ship's timber. Diving revealed the warship, which, though both bow and stern had collapsed, was sensationally intact and well away from the recorded position of her sinking in Navy records.

At first the site was thought to be that of *HMS Impregnable,* lost nearby (see Site 94), but a find by John Bingeman named her without any doubt. On the seabed he unfurled a piece of canvas sail still intact and protected by the mud. Inside the canvas written on a small wooden tag was: "Invincible. Flying Jib 26 x 26 No. 6"!

The *Invincible* was no ordinary ship. She was a prize. Built for the French Navy in 1741 by their master shipwright Morineau, she was far ahead of her time — better, faster and sounder than anything in service with the Royal Navy. She soon proved this, capturing *HMS Elizabeth,* taking on odds of four to one and winning. But even she could not cope with an entire squadron, who captured her off Cape Finisterre in 1747. Her capture is said to have led to a vital re-think in the building of British ships without which Nelson would not have won at Trafalgar years later.

Be that as it may, the advanced design of the *Invincible* did not save her from a series of mishaps on February 19, 1758. At 2.30a.m. Admiral Edward

Boscawen ordered the ship to up anchor and sail for Canada, where she was to take part in the campaign to oust the French.

That sudden order seems to have upset things on board the man o'war. The dark and the wind funnelling up the Solent from the east did not help, but soon there was no doubt that *Invincible* was having real problems.

By 0415 she had her anchor in a twist. By 0445 she finally got it catted and minutes later set off on a north-east course to get some sea room on the fast ebbing tide. It was then that her rudder jammed and she sailed straight on until she grounded hard. All efforts to free her failed. Three days later, with all the crew safely off and much of her cargo removed, a great wind came out of the west, she heeled and went on heeling until she was on her side. Water rushed in and she sank into the silt. Her Captain, John Bentley, was acquitted at the court-martial and the wreck was left there under the silt about one-and-a-half miles south-east of Horse Sand Fort.

Diving has recovered a host of items from the old ship and many can be seen in the Royal Navy Museum in Portsmouth.

96 M.F.V. 118. At 50 44 26; 01 03 19. Depth 6m. This wreck is probably the remains of the fishing vessel *M.F.V. 118*, although it is unknown when she sank. There was a report of a wreck in this position in 1945. Divers in 1976 reported that the wreck was an unidentified wooden craft which lay north-east and south-west and stood off the seabed around a metre. This was confirmed during recent diving.

The site lies just 100 yards to the south-east of the Horse Elbow Buoy and is very close to the wreck of the Cambrian (See 91).

Bembridge 2.5 miles; Portsmouth 3.5 miles.

97 Tank Landing Craft. At 50 43 39; 01 03 37. Depth 30m. This wreck was first located in May 1967 ¼ mile east of the Warner Buoy, and is in fact a large landing craft. It is upright and intact, and lies roughly north and south with the bows to the south. The site is around 50 yards long with a maximum height of 7m. The stern is very low, almost at the seabed level of the soft mud.

Visibility here can be exceptional – "The viz was so fantastic that when I was up on the bridge I could see the bow ramp quite clearly", said one diver recently. But be warned it is not often like that!

Bembridge 2 miles; Portsmouth 4 miles.

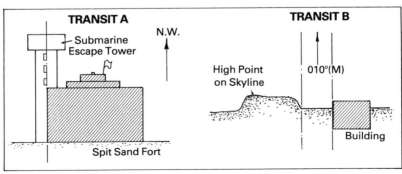

Marks for HMS Hazard. (Site 98).

Once a torpedo gunboat, HMS Hazard *became a submarine tender. She was rammed and sunk in 1918. Courtesy Tom Rayner.*

98 HMS Hazard. At 50 43 45; 01 03 14. Depth: 32m. *HMS Hazard* started life as a torpedo gunboat and was one of the Dryad class. She was launched in 1894 and displaced 1070-tons. She measured 250ft x 30ft x 13ft and had a complement of 120 men. She was well armed with 2-4.7m guns, 4-3pdr's and 5-18-inch torpedo tubes. She was driven by two sets of vertical triple expansion engines and could produce 3,500h.p. with a top speed of 18 knots.

With the introduction of Holland-class submarines into the Royal Navy in 1901, the need for a tender ship was obvious and the *Hazard* was appointed to this task.

On January 28, 1918 *Hazard* was rammed by the 2,937-ton casualty-clearing steamer *Western Australia* and cut in two. She sank very quickly with the loss of three lives. A fourth man died later from his injuries.

The *Hazard* is rarely visited by divers. She lies half a mile east of the Warner Buoy in the centre of the deep water channel leading into the Eastern Solent. This is an extremely busy part of the channel with many ferries, tankers and Naval ships coming and going all the time. Coupled with the strong tide and poor visibility normally found in the centre of the channel the dangers are obvious. The *Hazard* is almost totally upside down and well buried in the soft mud. Her bronze props are gone, salvaged some years ago. She is in half and the two parts lie alongside one another. The only connections between them are some cables, possibly from the salvage of the condensers in 1974.

Bembridge 2 miles; Portsmouth 4 miles.

99 Collier. At 50 43 37; 01 03 05. Depth: 28m. A collier of about 150ft long, she is sitting upright with her bows to the south-east on a bed of grey mud.

There is a one metre scour around her and she stands six metres proud. She is largely intact.

Bembridge 2.5 miles; Portsmouth 4.5 miles.

100 The Stone Wreck. At 50 43 26; 01 02 04. Depth: 20m. This site 3½ miles south of Langstone Harbour entrance is a bit of a mystery. The wreck appears to be just a rocky outcrop, but on closer inspection the rocks are large ballast sotones of a regular shape, and if you look closer still you will see some wooden timbers protruding from beneath the stones. The wreck lies north-west and south-east and is of a ship about 50ft long and 15ft beam. She stands up a maximum of 2m. There is a scour of half a metre deep around the outline of the hull. This is an old wreck, possibly a sailing barge. Divers have recovered a wooden pulley and a bronze fireplace.

N.B. The site lies in the centre of the deep water channel leading into the eastern Solent so care needs to be taken.

Bembridge 3 miles; Portsmouth 5 miles.

101 Concrete cylinder. At 50 43 27; 01 04 18. Depth: 10m. This obstruction is a cylindrical concrete structure about 100ft long and eight feet in diameter standing nearly two metres proud of the bottom of fine sand and mud. This is probably a petrol barge built for the Allied invasion of France. Each barge carried some 200 tons of petrol and some 200 of them were built. The concrete proved highly resistant to petrol and aviation spirit in particular. This one obviously did not make it across the Channel. Or it could be one of the "Sausages" (see next Site).

Bembridge 2 miles; Portsmouth 4 miles.

102 Sausages. On the Warner Shoal. Depth: 10m. The Warner Shoal covers a large area from the eastern side of Ryde Sands round to St. Helen's Roads, marked to the north by the Warner Buoy and No Man's Land Fort. The obstructions, whose shape has earned them the name of "Sausages", are of two kinds. During WW2 a submarine defence system was deployed between the Island and the Southsea Shore to prevent German submarines doing a "Royal Oak" on warships anchored at Spithead. This system used big concrete cylinders with a diameter of over seven feet. They varied in length from 36 to 150ft. After the war many of them were sunk and they can be found scattered around the Warner Shoal. But some of the obstructions here are of the second kind – bombardons. The Bombardon Floating Breakwaters were part of the Mulberry Harbours in France. These bombardons broke the waves – even in winds of over Force 6 – and enabled small boats to work unloading supplies as soon as they were in place on the coast of France on D-Day Plus Three. Made of quarter-inch mild steel with watertight buoyancy compartments, the breakwaters were moored in several fathoms of water to give sufficient depth for Liberty ships to anchor behind them. Two miles of Bombardon Breakwater was used in the actual D-Day operations. Those on the Warner Shoal presumably broke away during towing to France.

The larger sections of both kinds of wreckage – all a favourite haunt of crab and lobster – can be found in the following positions: At 50 43 56; 01 05 19. At 50 43 39; 01 04 38. At 50 43 27; 01 04 18. And at 50 43 20; 01 05 24.

Bembridge 1.5 miles; Portsmouth 3.5 miles.

103 Obstruction. At 50 43 13; 01 04 34. Depth: 9m. This is in fact a small pontoon in three sections about 12 feet square and bolted together to make a structure some 40ft by 10ft by 12ft. There is another one on its side and slightly smaller about half a mile to the west.

Bembridge 1 mile; Portsmouth 5 miles.

104 Obstruction. At 50 43 02; 01 02 48. Depth: 16m. This obstruction was first reported in 1968 and was believed to have been a large load of spoil dumped in rough weather. The position is 1.5 miles north-east of St. Helen's Fort and it stands 1-2m proud of the seabed with a length of around 20 yards.

This site was located recently and dived by Mike Walsh, who confirmed that it was indeed a mound of mud and clay. There was no sign of any wreckage and no magnetometer reading was obtained.

Bembridge 2 miles; Portsmouth 5 miles.

105 UB-21. At 50 44 14; 01 01 31. Depth: 5m. This veteran German submarine of WW1 came to an inglorious end when on her way to the breakers in 1920. She sank while under tow three miles south of Eastney Point.

UB-21 was one of the smaller U-boats, 292 tons, 118ft long, with a crew of two officers and 21 men. She had two bow tubes and carried four torpedoes and an 8cm gun on her casing. She was launched in 1916 and was one of 176 U-boats which were surrendered at the end of the war.

At one period of her long service, the *UB-21* was commanded by the burly, jovial Kapitanleutnant Ernst Hashagen. Hashagen who also survived the war, was rated as an "ace" in the scoring table of the U-boat commands,, having sunk over 130,000 tons of Allied shipping during his North Sea and Channel missions in *UB-21* and his later boat, *U-62.*

It was when in command of *UB-21* that Ernst Hashagen took a leading part in one of the strangest incidents of the submarine war. He described it like this:

"There was the little steamer *Fritzoe.* We met her in the North Sea and sent a shot from the gun of *UB-21* ripping over her bow. She hove-to and I signalled the captain to bring over his papers. He came, but I needed only one look at his battered lifeboats to know that his crew could never make it

This group of submarines at Portsmouth after WW1 includes UB21.

to the nearest land. The question was, what to do with the ship now that I had her? The expression on the captain's face told me he was wondering the same thing. I had an idea.

"Look here," I turned to him, "You may take your choice of having your ship sunk here or of taking her to Cuxhaven on your own as a war prize. Which shall it be?" You never saw such a look of relief on the face of a man. Without hesitation he agreed to take the *Fritzoe* to Germany.

"But how do I know you will do as you say?" I asked him. "I can't follow you all the time. I must watch out for British patrol boats. There is nothing to prevent you from trying to give me the slip. Then I would have to shoot a torpedo at you. No, perhaps I had better sink you right here."

"The captain turned a bit pale, but stood his ground. "I am a man of my word," he said with fine dignity. We parted and I lost sight of the steamer. I never really expected to see it again. Four days later when I reached Cuxhaven, there was the *Fritzoe* waiting for us. That Britisher knew how to play cricket. All honour to him. His word was his bond!"

The *UB-21* was depth-charged many times in her active wartime career and always managed to escape, but demolition teams in 1921 and salvage work in 1970, when she was sold to a Portsmouth firm, succeeded where the Allied Navies had failed. She is now very broken and dispersed. The wreck is in two sections and much flattened so that just a few isolated plates stick up some two metres off the bottom.

Bembridge is 3.5 miles; Portsmouth 4.5 miles.

106 The Broad Arrow Wreck. At 50 46 17; 00 59 52. Depth: 3m. The remains of a steel wreck located by divers in 1985, the site is in shallow water about a quarter-of-a-mile off the beach at Hayling Island just to the east of the East Winner Sand.

The wreck is small in extent and very low, and is well covered in silt. No sign of any machinery was found but an engine room repeater was discovered marked with the Royal Navy's broad arrow, which would indicate a naval vessel of some sort. From the size and type of fittings seen on the wreck it would seem that her original size would have been about 100ft long.

Bembridge 6 miles; Portsmouth 4.5 miles.

107 Church Rocks. At 50 45 36; 00 59 14. Depth: 3m. This small rocky outcrop was thought to be just that until Alexander McKee and Maurice Harknett discovered the reason for the name. Their finds of ancient stonework has confirmed the belief of historians that this is the site of a priory church and village submerged in the 14th century. The rocks can be very kelpy, are a mark for local spear fishermen, and a good site for shellfish.

Bembridge 6 miles; Portsmouth 5 miles.

108 Caduceus. At 50 45 51; 00 57 58. Depth: 3m. The barque *Caduceus* was 124ft long and was wrecked on October 23, 1881 approximately three-quarters-of-a-mile to the west of Chichester Bar.

The 405-ton ship having grounded in shallow water was quickly broken up by the sea and some parts of her were still to be seen at Low Water until the 1950's.

It was not until 1970 that the site was investigated by divers. They were able to identify the ship after finding part of her bell which was dated 1837.

This British-designed submarine sank in 1904 after she was rammed. Later repaired, she exploded in 1910 and in 1911 became a target.

Little is left of the ship now. One of the highest parts is a galvanised iron tank which stands about half a metre off the seabed.

The *Caduceus* was used as a sailing collier towards the end of her days. The keel and some bronze bolts can be seen on the site together with a few timbers in good conditions and the odd iron fitting.

Bembridge 6 miles; Portsmouth 6 miles.

109 H.M. Submarine A-1. At 50 44 00; 01 06 00. Position is approximate but close. Depth: 5m. The submarine *A-1* was the first British-designed submarine to follow the Navy's initial use of American-designed Holland-class boats built in this country. A-1 was just 100ft long and weighed 165 tons. She was laid down on February 19, 1902 in the Vickers and Maxim yard at Barrow-in-Furness and was launched on July 9, 1902. She cost £41,000.

A-1 was to become Britain's first submarine disaster. In March 1904 she and some Holland class subs were taking part in manoeuvres which included mock attacks on various Naval ships. *A-1* was commanded by Lieutenant Loftus Mansergh. He had lined up his submarine for an attack on the cruiser *Juno* and was unaware that the liner *Berwick Castle* was steaming out to sea on her way from Southampton to Hamburg. The captain of the *Berwick Castle* saw something ahead of him in the water and rang for full astern and put his helm hard a'starboard, but it was too late and he struck the sub a shattering blow which sent her to the seabed. Even then the officers on the liner thought that they had hit a practice torpedo and not a partially-submerged submarine.

The sunken submarine was soon located by a steady stream of air bubbles from her, but several attempts at raising her failed. A month later she was raised and her crew of 11 buried. She was put back into service after repairs, but little more was heard of her by the outside world until August 1910 when a huge explosion took place on board her as she was alongside at Portsmouth. Seven men were badly hurt. One man, the cox'n, was actually blown out through the conning-tower and landed in the sea. The explosion was caused by an accumulation of petrol gas inside her from the fuel for her engines.

In August 1911, the *A-1* was towed out of Portsmouth to be used as a gunnery target. Her position when sunk was given as half-a-mile south-west of No Man's Land Fort but the towing ship failed to pinpoint her position.

She was found after being snagged by trawlerman Willie Pledger of Selsey and then dived by Chichester sub-aqua club.

Bembridge 2 miles; Portsmouth 3.5 miles.

110 Shallom. At 50 47 00; 00 59 42. Depth: 10m. This is the remains of a 20ft cabin cruiser which sank on May 24, 1983 after striking some submerged object. Very broken.

Bembridge 6 miles; Portsmouth 4.5 miles.

111 The Net Wreck. At 50 42 56; 01 01 58. Depth: 15m. This wreck, name unknown, has been trawled into so often that it is sometimes difficult to see the ship for the nets. She was first dived in 1980 and divers found a small vessel of about 30 feet long in the position some two miles north-east of St. Helens Fort. They also reported more wreckage scattered over the seabed with the largest item a box-like structure standing one-and-a-half metres proud. This is possibly another Unifloat (See Site 54). They concluded that there was even more wreckage buried under the mud. A magnetometer survey of the site produces strong anomalies, but on diving only bits of girderwork are to be found. There is even more wreckage further to the west and local divers believe that this comes from a much bigger vessel which was dispersed many years ago. All the wreckage is good for shellfish.

Bembridge 2.5 miles; Portsmouth 5.5 miles.

112 The Big Box. At 50 43 00; 01 01 48. Depth: 14m. This unusual piece of wreckage is three-quarters-of-a-mile north-west of the Nab East Buoy. A large box section about the size of a large car, it stands almost 2m high and is very strongly built. It lays in a north-east south-west direction on the side

Small coaster Capable, *hit a mine off Bembridge in 1940, after an earlier near-wreck in 1930.*

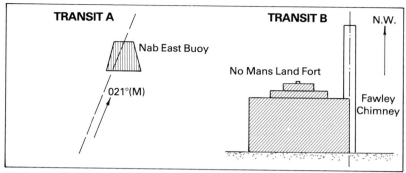

Marks for Capable. (Site 113).

of a bank and is probably part of the D-Day debris in the area.
Bembridge 3 miles; Portsmouth 5 miles.

113 Capable. At 50 42 46; 01 00 46. Depth: 14m. The M.V. *Capable* was a small coaster of 216 tons, which for many years sailed between south coast ports both east and west of the Isle of Wight. Her first attempt at becoming a local wreck was on March 3, 1930. Shortly after leaving Poole harbour, she was passing along the back of the Isle of Wight, when she ran into thick fog. At 2230 hours she ran aground on the infamous Atherfield Ledges. Luckily the Coastguard lookout had seen her plight and a stout rope was soon rigged and all the crew were able to scramble to safety. Word of the stranding was soon out and the two lifeboats from Brook and Yarmouth were launched. The Brook boat eventually found the *Capable* but only after the crew had already left. The Yarmouth lifeboat only reached Brook Ledge before running aground herself. She was there for several days before a party of troops were able to refloat her.

The *Capable*, although badly damaged was refloated and towed to Cowes where she was repaired.

The *Capable* finally became a permanent wreck on June 5, 1940 when she hit a mine off Bembridge and sank just to the south of the Nab East Buoy. She was bringing a cargo of stone from Alderney to Portsmouth. She had a crew of five and two Territorial Army gunners on board and all were lost.

The site today is well broken up, mainly a mass of steel plates and ribs. One of her anchors can be seen within the wreckage. On one dive recently three navigation lamps were found well jammed under some plates. One was eventually rescued but the other two are still there.

Bearing from the Horse Sand Fort is 131 degrees, 2.8 miles, and from St. Helen's Fort 80 degrees, 2.72 miles.

Bembridge 3 miles; Portsmouth 6 miles.

114 The German Tug. At 50 42 47; 00 59 33. Depth: 23m. First found in 1957, this ship's real name is unknown, but veteran local diver Maurice Harknett called her the German Tug after studying her remains very carefully. The wreck is broken, but her bows are complete, though the rest of her is split open. Her two boilers are well proud and the steel propellor still in place. It is an interesting fin from the bow, where the anchors are still in their hawses, to the stern which is deep in the mud. There is plenty of coal amid the wreckage and a big winch and a large rope roller, some six feet long, give strength to the identification of her as a tug. Some bottles have been recovered from the wreck. One had the date of February, 1922 moulded into the glass. There is a great deal of broken German pottery in the wreckage. This is a good dive as the viz is often surprisingly good with over 10m not uncommon. A recent recovery from the wreck were three bronze dolphins, which possibly held a compass bowl.

N.B. The wreck lies on the edge of the deep water channel for ships heading into the Eastern Solent and is just 400 yards north-west of the Nab End Buoy, so take care.

Bembridge 4 miles; Portsmouth 6.5 miles.

115 The Lobster Pockets. At 50 42 50; 01 01 15. Depth: 14m. This "unknown" is a small wreck about 60ft long, standing a metre proud and lying almost east to west. She is upside down or seems to be with her iron keel lying across the top. Twin iron props are still there. Only the outline of the sides of the wreck can be seen from the wood sticking up some two feet from the mud in a ship shape. It is an excellent site for lobsters and looking down on her from above the lobsters look as though they are in pockets – made by the internal bulkheads of the old ship!

Bembridge 2½ miles; Portsmouth 5½ miles.

116 German E-Boat. At 50 42 45; 00 56 24 1. Depth: 15m. This site is the remains of a German E-Boat which sank here during WW2 after being holed 4 miles south of Eastoke Point. The site was surveyed in 1951 and the wreck was dispersed the same year.

Today the remains of the wreck lie in a crater and very little of her sticks above the rim. The wreck itself is now very flat. The maximum height of isolated parts is only 1m at best. Nothing is really recognisable, but the site is still worth a rummage. The surrounding seabed is fairly flat and mainly sand and shingle. A small gun was recovered in 1972.

Bembridge 6 miles; Portsmouth 8 miles.

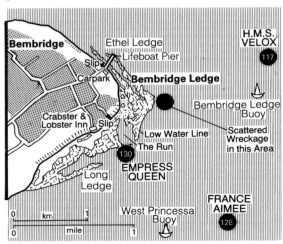

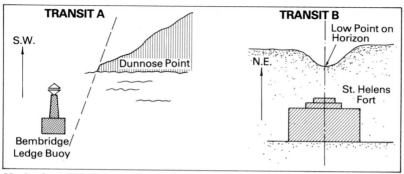

Marks for HMS Velox. (Site 117).

117 HMS Velox. At 50 41 31; 01 02 05. Depth: 13m. This British destroyer was one of the three first Royal Navy ships to be fitted with steam turbines. These revolutionary new engines, the invention of Sir Charles Algernon Parsons, were to change the whole face of naval warfare. Suddenly it was possible for ships to reach undreamed of speeds and to be reliable too. The Navy raced to fit them in their latest ships.

First of them all was *HMS Viper*. Her 10,000hp engines could shove her through the sea at the astounding speed of 36.58 knots. She was 210ft long, but only 21ft wide and drew just 12.5ft, despite the fact that she mounted a 12-pdr gun, five 6-pdrs and two torpedo tubes. Her engines worked by a jet of steam being directed on to angled blades on a drum connected either directly or through gearing to the propellor shaft. The power to weight ratio, compared with the old steam-reciprocating engines, was so favourable that all the navies of the world started to adopt the system.

The *Viper* was the first of the Snake-class and was, at that time, the fastest thing afloat. But her shallow draught tended to make her ride on bow and

The stern lamp from HMS Velox, *one of the first steam turbine destroyers.*

95

stern waves with her midships almost suspended out of the water. Her stability in sharp turns was questionable. The *Viper* did not last long. She ran on to the Renonquet Reef off Alderney during manoeuvres with the Fleet on August 3, 1901.

Next to be built of the Snake-class was *HMS Cobra*. She too could do over 36 knots and her draught was even less – just seven feet. Before she was completely ready for Naval service she needed some adjustments during sea trials. For that reason there were 25 men, including the manager, of Parsons Marine Steam Turbine Company aboard when she left Newcastle in the evening of Tuesday, September 17, 1901. Already on board were the Navy crew of 54 men.

At 4a.m. the next day she ran into a full gale and the midsection was heard creaking under the strain of only being supported at bow and stern. In addition, she rolled heavily. At 7.30a.m. she simply broke in two. Only 12 men survived.

There was now a great public outcry – some thought the snake names unlucky and the steam turbines too powerful, for surely here was evidence that they tore ships in two!

The Admiralty, to their credit, took little notice and continued to believe in the steam turbine engines. But they did think it wise to change the name of the third Snake-class boat from *Python* to *Velox*.

The *Velox* was launched in 1902 and completed in February, 1904, and she stayed *HMS Velox,* a C-Class destroyer, throughout her Navy service. She was a 420-ton ship 210ft long with a beam of 21ft and a draught of 9ft. She had her 12-pdr gun just forward of the bridge, two 6-pdrs on each side and one aft, and two 18in torpedo tubes. The turbines drove four propshafts, each fitted with two propellors, but this arrangement was later modified to only one propellor per shaft.

She was vastly important in her service. She served her time with no problems of any note and demonstrated that steam turbines were not too powerful and were reliable. And she was still proving that on October 25, 1915 when she hit a mine laid by a German UC-class submarine of the Flanders Flotilla near the Nab Tower. The *Velox* finally sank one-and-a-half miles east of Bembridge Lifeboat Station.

In 1970, the wreck was bought by a salvage company and they well and truly dispersed her. Today she is still an interesting dive. Her propshafts are still there and so are parts of her turbines, but none of the hull shows above the muddy seabed. As the wreckage is so widely scattered, it does pay to explore away from the main site and many souvenirs can still be found.

Bembridge 3 miles; Portsmouth 7.5 miles.

118 Mooring Block. At 50 41 30; 01 02 19. Depth: 12m. Don't bother diving – this is only a 2 yard square concrete mooring block with two large steel rings set into the sides. It is one of several mooring blocks used by the salvage vessel working the site of *HMS Velox*. This is probably the largest and can be found some distance from the main wreckage.

Bembridge 3 miles; Portsmouth 7.5 miles.

119 Obstruction. At 50 41 17; 01 01 44. Depth: 11m. A small obstruction was located in this position 1½ miles east of Bembridge lifeboat station in 1979. It was reported that it was about 5ft long, lay north-east, south-west and stood a maximum of 1m off the bottom.

Bembridge 2½ miles; Portsmouth 8 miles.

120 Unknown. At 50 41 01; 01 01 32. Depth: 12m. A small wreck is in this position 1½ miles east of Forelands. She is about 30ft long and stands 1m high. She is barge shaped, lies east to west and is well broken.
Bembridge 2½ miles; Portsmouth 7½ miles.

121 Unknown. At 50 41 21. 01 00 06. Depth: 13m. This wreck, 2½ miles east of Bembridge lifeboat station is a mystery. It was first located in 1945 and dived on by Navy divers who reported finding a small steel craft about 40' long with a 12' beam, with some wooden decking in places. The ship was badly damaged and they saw what appeared to be a drifter type winch forward and roller fairleads at the stern. Lying just clear of the wreck was a small gun and mounting and an anchor with a 4ft shank.

Subsequent surveys of the area failed to find any trace of the wreck until 1979 when an obstruction was seen during a sonar sweep. It stood 3m off the seabed and was very small.

The site was dived on recently and it was difficult to recognise anything except that on one length of plate there was three portholes. Two had only the bases left, still well bolted, and one was complete. Also well buried was what looked like a large brass shell case. A large badly damaged navigation lamp was recovered and this and the other items all seemed rather large to have been fitted on a small 40ft craft. It is possible that this in fact is only a part of a ship. No sign was seen of the gun and anchor found in 1945.

Some of the fitting raised from this site are "high class" which makes divers think that this may be part of the anti-submarine yacht *Campeador V,* which was beached near here after being mined (See Site 133).
Bembridge 3.5 miles; Portsmouth 7 miles.

122 Sir Jasper. At 50 42 12; 00 57 00. Depth: 13m. Another victim of Solent racing, this J-24 Class yacht capsized and sank while overtaking another yacht on November 1, 1981 near the Nab No. 3 Buoy. Position is approximate. Diving information required.
Bembridge 5.5 miles; Portsmouth 8.5 miles.

123 Obstruction. At 50 41 36; 00 56 42. Depth: 11m. This was a very small obstruction on the edge of the dredged Nab Channel and it has not been located by divers for some time. This leads them to believe that the obstruction has been destroyed or covered by recent dredging operations in the area.
Bembridge 5.5 miles; Portsmouth 8.5 miles.

124 Unknown. At 50 40 15; 00 56 36. Depth: 15m. A pottery dish is the only clue to this "unknown", which was first located one third of a mile to the north-east of the Nab Tower in 1969. The site was dived in 1978 and the divers reported finding an old wooden steamship. The hull was mostly broken up and covered only a small area. The highest point was the boiler which stands about 3m off the bottom which is mainly sand and broken shells. The propeller is still there, a large four bladed one, made of steel with a diameter of approximately 7ft. The wreck lies north-east and south-west with its bows to the north-east. A dish recovered from the site had the inscription "made expressly for the United States Lines" on it.
Bembridge 6 miles; Portsmouth 9.5 miles.

125 Nab Tower. At 50 40 00; 00 57 00. The tower is at the southern end of

This amazing structure, **The Nab** *once called "the Wedding Cake ship", planted in the Solent in 1920, was originally designed as part of a Dover Straits anti-submarine barrier. (Site 125).*

the eastern approach to Spithead and Portsmouth and stands 28m high. It has been responsible for guiding ships into the deep water channel since it was set in place on Sunday, September 12, 1920.

The story of the Nab starts in 1917, when attacks on British and Allied merchant shipping by the U-boats of the Flanders Flotilla based at Bruges, reached such a rate of sinkings that Britain faced starvation. These German U-boats would slip out of Zeebrugge, usually at night, and run the gauntlet of mines and nets with which the British Admiralty tried to close the Dover Straits, and play havoc with shipping in the Channel. Something more was obviously needed – and a hastily convened "Barrage Committee" of scientists and sailors finally came up with the idea which they thought could provide the ultimate in anti-submarine operations. Six enormous towers were to be built and sunk in position across the Straits of Dover. These forts would be the supports for huge steel nets reaching from seabed to surface and once in position no U-boat would pass.

At least that was the idea. Work began at once on two of the towers at Southwick, near Shoreham in Sussex. Each was to be 40ft in diameter, with latticed steelwork surrounding the 28m high cylindrical steel tower. This was to be set upon a huge concrete base, designed like a honeycomb for flooding and sinking in water of 20 fathoms. The base was roughly shaped with pointed bows and stern for easy towing.

Some 3,000 civilian workmen were brought to Southwick, chosen for its huge supplies of shingle for the concrete, and work began under a strict veil of secrecy. Despite this as the towers grew they became known in the Navy as the "Southwick Monsters" or "The Wedding Cake Ships".

The work was supervised by the Royal Engineers, but only one tower was completed when the war ended in November, 1918 and the other –

half-finished – was broken up and scrapped.

The great tower stayed on shore until Trinity House decided to replace the old Nab Lightship. Then on September 12, 1920 – chosen because it was flat calm – two aged paddlesteamer tugs towed the huge structure to a position near the Light vessel. And, as the base was opened to the sea, the tower performed exactly as planned and settled almost gently to the seabed. This was, of course, much to the relief of the civilian who had designed it, Mr. G. Menzies.

The Nab Tower is four-and-a-half miles east of Bembridge and six miles south of Chichester Harbour entrance and operated as a manned offshore lighthouse from the time of its sinking until quite recently. It used to be staffed by three keepers who were relieved every month, but now it is automated and the tower and its helicopter landing pad is serviced and monitored from East Cowes.

The height of the light is 27m. It has an intensity of 100,000 candela, group flashing white every 10 seconds and can be seen 19 miles away. In fog there are two blasts every 30 seconds. Over the years the tower has developed a slight list of two degrees and has moved two feet since 1920.

Diving the Nab is interesting. The concrete base goes down in three steps. Each step is five metres high and two metres wide. These steps drop down to the sand and shingle seabed at 20m. The base is a favourite haunt of crab and lobster. Diving can be carried out at anytime as a lee from the tide can be found at some point around the base.

A rocky ridge with much life – depth 13m – lies 600 yards north-east of the Tower.

Bembridge 6 miles; Portsmouth 9 miles.

Nab Channel. Divers should be alert to the fact that the Nab Channel, which is over 400 yards wide, starts about a mile north-north-east of the Nab Tower and extends one-and-a-half miles north-north-west from that point. It is dredged to a depth of 13m and is intended for heavily-laden inward-bound tankers. All other boats should keep clear of the channel.

126 Bettann (Stern). At 50 40 17; 01 00 57. Depth: 13m. The Danish coaster *Bettann* under the comand of Captain Petersen was on a voyage from Cornwall to Germany with a cargo of china clay, valued at £35,000. The 500-ton ship started to leak badly while heading up the English Channel and when the electric bilge pumps failed, the crew of five men and one woman began bailing with buckets. Some 24 hours after the leak started the Destroyer *HMS Agincourt* took the *Bettann* in tow. She was finally anchored in shallow water in St. Helen's Roads. The Bembridge lifeboat was standing by and as the water began to rise over the hatches the crew abandoned ship. Shortly afterwards, she rolled over and sank. The date was January 19, 1967.

Attempts to raise the wreck failed and eventually she was cut into two sections. These sections were then raised and towed out to deep water to be sunk again for good. The stern section, however, never made it to the deep water; she sank while being towed 2½ miles west of the Nab Tower on December 4, 1968.

The stern section is small, only about 15 yards long and stands a maximum of 5m off the sand and gravel seabed. A couple of portholes were recovered by local divers shortly after she sank, but nothing of interest has shown since then. Angling boats often visit this site and many lose their

Two alone...girl cook and fiancé fight to save sinking coaster

STAY-ON IRIS

By JACK HILL

THE ship was sinking. But pretty Iris Larsen clung on desperately yesterday, refusing to leave the doomed vessel.

For also aboard was the man she loves — Captain Mogens Petersen.

And when the rest of the crew had left the Danish coaster Bettann, 22-year-old Iris, ship's cook as well as the captain's fiancee, stayed with him on the steeply listing deck.

Finally, just before the Bettann sank in St. Helena Roads, off the Isle of Wight, the captain ordered her off.

Iris, exhausted after battling with her shipmates for 40 hours to try to save the ship jumped overboard and joined the rest of the crew in the Bembridge lifeboat.

After her, at the Bettann heeled again, leaped Captain Petersen. Three minutes later the vessel sank.

BATTLE TO SAVE BLOOD CHANGE BABY FAILS

By JAMES WILKINSON

THE unborn baby whose blood was changed in a rare operation was feared last night to have died.

"There is no sign that the baby is still alive," said a spokesman from St. Bartholomew's Hospital, London.

The midwife's condition remains excellent. It is, however, feared that the tube to the baby has attacked inside the womb, so that direct treatment could not be continued."

The blood had to be changed because it was not compatible with the mother's. Without the change the baby was doomed.

'I'm so proud'

The Daily Express features the romance between the Captain and the cook of the Bettann.

anchors, so if you're an anchor collecter — this may be the spot for you!
The forward section of the *Bettann* is in this book at Site 160.

127 Unknown. At 50 40 08; 01 02 50. Depth: 13m. An obstruction located in the centre of the Princessa Shoal. It is reported to stand 1½m high and is small in extent, possibly a little boat. This site is 1½ miles east of Culver Cliff. Diving information required.
Bembridge 2.5 miles; Portsmouth 7.5 miles.

128 France Aimee. At 50 40 05; 01 03 16. Depth: 13m. This could well be called the ship which fell into a hole. For this French collier of 699 tons, which sank on April 3, 1918 after a collision with one of the Royal Navy's P-class patrol boats, *HMS P-35,* at first lay on the seabed on the northern edge of a large hole. And then she rolled into it!
The *France Aimee* was built in 1901 by the Irvine Shipbuilding Company and was owned at the time of the collision by the Societe D'Importation du Nord et De L'Est. She was 190ft long with a beam of 28ft and built of steel

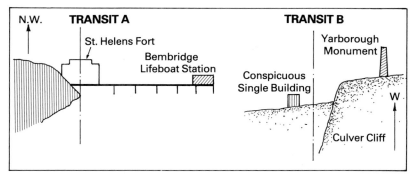

Marks for the France Aimeé. (Site 128).

with a single deck. The *P-35* of 613 tons, 230ft long, which carried a 4-inch gun and two torpedo tubes, was built by Caird in January, 1917 and survived the collision. She carried on with the Navy after repairs until she was broken up in Plymouth in January, 1923.

The collision took place in appalling weather and very low visibility. When the *France Aimee* sank she was on the western edge of the Princessa Shoal about 400 yards to the east of the Princessa Shoal Buoy. When first dived in 1964 she was heavily covered with big mussels and weed and tilted to port on the edge of a large hole or dip in the seabed. By 1972 she had rolled over into the middle of the hole and was now completely on her port side. Today divers will find her with her stern intact, her port side all silted up, with her starboard side collapsed, leaving her boiler clear and the highest point at three metres. The bows are almost buried, but intact with one anchor still neatly stowed. Many piles of coal, her cargo, lie on the seabed around the site. There is a three metre scour around some of the wreckage. A porthole was raised last year.

Bembridge 2.5 miles; Portsmouth 7.5 miles.

129 Bembridge Ledge. Bembridge Ledge is another favourite area for diving. Not surprising as huge numbers of crab and lobster abound among the large slabs of rock that stretch out from the shore as far as the Bembridge Ledge Buoy, which is almost a mile offshore. At Low Water the rocks are dry for more than a quarter mile offshore. Many ships, including a submarine, have spent some time aground on the ledges after trying to cut the corner too close. Luckily most of them escaped with little damage. The paddle steamer *Empress Queen* did not. Parts of her can be seen at Low Water (See Site 130).

Due to the large number of crabs and lobsters found on the ledges, there are also a huge number of pots laid here. Great care must be taken to avoid them. The deeper part of the ledges – out towards the Ledge Buoy, are a good area for drift diving. There always seems to be a large number of anchors to be found caught up in the rocky slabs. This is because the ledge is also a favourite place for local angling. The depths near to the buoy are around 15m. Several old ships lave been lost in the area so you never know what you will come across. For example, Island diver Dougie Saunders found the remains of one wreck – "I was drift diving, and came across a fair sized propshaft complete with prop, as well as an old steam boiler and bits and pieces that looked as if they had come from a steam driven vessel of some sort."

One part of the ledge known as "The Run" is popular for snorkelling. This is a shallow channel which meanders between the rocks. The water is usually very clear and there is an abundant marine life.

On Long Ledge itself there are two big lagoons or rock pools full of crystal clear water near Foreland, which are used by Dave Ellison of the Isle of Wight School of Diving to introduce the disabled to sea diving.

130 Empress Queen. At 50 40 36; 01 04 00. Depth: 3m. The *Empress Queen* was a 1995-ton paddle steamer built in 1897 by the Fairfield Shipbuilding and Engineering Co. She was one of the most powerful paddlers of the period with engines producing some 10,000h.p. For many years she was owned and operated by the Isle of Man Ferry Co. During WW1, she was employed as a troop carrier. On February 3, 1916, she ran aground on the rocks of the Bembridge Ledge with over 100 men on board.

Bembridge Ledge claimed the Empress Queen, *a powerful paddle steamer built in 1897. Courtesy of Tom Rayner.*

The Bembridge lifeboat, the *Queen Victoria,* was launched with great difficulty, but she was soon able to reach the stricken steamer and promptly began to take off the troops and crew. Two full boatloads were taken and safely landed ashore. On the third trip out the lifeboat was driven on to the rocks herself suffering some damage but was still able to continue the rescue. In all 110 men, a cat and a dog were rescued. The coxswain John Holbrook was awarded the R.N.L.I.'s silver medal for the rescue.

The *Empress Queen* ended her days on the Bembridge Ledge gradually breaking up over the years. Most of the remains are well broken up and scattered around the rocks. At low water parts of her can be seen sticking out of the water and she is still a danger to small craft navigating close in.

Bembridge 2 miles; Portsmouth 7.5 miles.

131 HMS P.12 (Bow section). At 50 40 15; 01 05 30. Depth: 2m. Part of the bow section of this fast patrol boat of WW1 is sometimes uncovered when the beach gets a storm lashing. It is hardly a dive, but the stern section – she was cut clean in half in a collision on November 4, 1918 – is something else! See Site No. 141.

Bembridge 3 miles; Portsmouth 8 miles.

132 LCT-529. At 50 41 45; 01 04 51. Depth: 6m. This 200-ton tank landing craft sank a mile from the Nab Tower, but was raised and dumped in the present position. This is a Mark IV LCT with a length of 187ft and a beam of 39ft. She drew just 4 feet.

Bembridge 1 mile; Portsmouth 6 miles.

133 Campeador V. At 50 41 53; 01 04 59. Depth: 5m. This 213-ton anti-submarine yacht was mined on June 22, 1940 some two miles north-west of the Nab Tower. She was beached in her present position and is very broken in very shallow water. See Site 121.

Bembridge 1 mile; Portsmouth 6 miles.

Area Information and services

Admiralty Charts: 2045 (Outer Approaches to the Solent). 394 (The Solent – Eastern part). 2635 (Approaches to Portsmouth). 2050 (Eastern Approaches to the Solent). 3418 (Langstone and Chichester Harbours). 2631 (Portsmouth Harbour).
Ordnance Survey: 196.
Local Weather: (0898) 500403. Marinecall (0898) 500457. For mid-channel forecast. Southampton Weather Centre. Southampton (0703) 28844.
Local coastguard: 999 (emergencies). At sea VHF Channel 16. Solent Coastguard, Lee-On-Solent (0705) 552100.
Local BS-AC Branches: Aldershot Dolphins No. 60 hold their dry meetings at Rushmoor Rugby Football Club, Tile Barn Close, Farnborough, Hants on Thursdays from 21.00 onward. Wet meetings are held at Rushmoor Recreation Centre, Farnborough on Tuesdays from 9p.m. to 10.30p.m.

Alton Branch No. 798 hold both their dry and wet meetings at the Alton Sports Centre, Alton, Hants on Tuesdays. Dry meetings are on Tuesday from 7.30p.m. and wet meetings start there at 9p.m. Divers can usually be found in the Sports Centre bar on Tuesdays. The branch welcomes visiting divers to join them on dives. Contact: Bordon (04203) 5437 or 5513. The branch owns two inflatables.

Gosport and Fareham Branch No. 1015 hold dry meetings at St. Vincent Centre, Mill Lane, Gosport at 7p.m. on Thursdays and wet meetings follow the same evening in the Centre's pool at 8p.m. Visiting divers, who are welcome, can find the Gosport divers in the Queen Charlotte, Forton Road, Gosport after 9p.m. on Thursdays. To join the branch on dives contact Ian Duffield Gosport (0705) 523592. The branch own a converted assault craft and an inflatable.

Southdown Divers Branch No. 1430 hold their dry meetings prior to wet meetings, which are at Wakeford's School pool, Wakeford's Way, Havant, Hants on Tuesdays from 9p.m. to 10p.m. Afterwards they can be found in The Fountain, Rowlands Castle. Visiting divers are welcome.

Southsea Branch No. 9 is a veteran, large and very active branch with its own clubhouse on the Ground Floor, Great Salterns Mansion, Eastern Road, Portsmouth. This is open on Tuesday and Thursday evenings from 7.30p.m. Dry meetings are held here and the clubhouse is open to visiting divers who are welcomed. Wet meetings are at the Victoria Pool, Anglesey Road, Portsmouth on Thursdays from 9-10p.m. Visiting divers are able to join branch dives if room available. Contact Portsmouth (0705) 828310. The branch own three inflatables, and a compressor (see Air supplies).

Accommodation: Details from Portsmouth Tourist Information Centre, The Hard, Portsmouth, Hants. Tel: Portsmouth (0705) 826722. And Hayling Island Tourist Information Centre, The Seafront, Hayling Island. Tel: Hayling Island (0705) 467111. For Isle of Wight accommodation see Area Three.

Air supplies: At Aldershot. From Aldershot Dolphins. Thursdays May to September 8-9p.m. Contact: Geoff Martin (0252) 876414.

At Alton. From Alton BS-AC at Alton Sports Centre. Contact Bordon (04203) 5437 or 5513.

At Portsmouth. From Southsea Branch. At their clubhouse, Ground Floor, Great Salterns Mansion, Eastern Road, Portsmouth. For filling times contact Portsmouth (0705) 828310.

At Southsea. Peter Anderson Sports Ltd., 48-50, Elm Grove, Southsea, Portsmouth. Tel: Portsmouth (0705) 820611. Air to 3000 psi. Fully-stocked dive shop also testing and servicing. Open Mons to Sats 9a.m. to 6p.m.

At Portsmouth. Solent Divers, 122-128, Lake Road, Portsmouth. Tel: Portsmouth (0705) 814924. Air to 4,000 psi. Manufacturer of suits, also fully-stocked dive shop, testing and servicing. Open Mon to Sat 8a.m.-6p.m.

At Gosport. Ocean Marine and Technical Services, Camper and Nicholson Marina, Mumby Road, Gosport, Hants. Tel: Gosport (0705) 529843. Evenings: Titchfield (0329) 42760. Air to 4,000 psi. Open Mon to Sat, office hours. OMTS offers professional diving services. Diving Services (Isle of Wight): Solent and Wight Diving Services, Duver Road, Seaview, Isle of Wight PO34 5AJ. Tel: (0983) 812033, mobile (0860) 526231. Sales, servicing, hire and instruction. Air.

Outboard Services: At Eastney. Ron Hale Marine, 94-98 Highland Road, Eastney, Hants. Tel: Portsmouth (0705) 732985. Repairs all leading makes of outboards and depot for inflatable repairs. At Emsworth. A.R. Savage Limited, Emsworth Yacht Harbour, Emsworth. And at Hayling Island in Sparkes Marina, Wittering Road, Hayling Island, Hants. Repairs all makes of outboards and marine engines. Tel: (0705) 469131.

Boats for Hire:

At Emsworth: *Portsmouth Diver* (Diver-skipper Walter Kennedy) 12 divers, 32ft, all electronic gear. Tel: (0243) 371292.

At Gosport: *Hero* (Skippers Jan and Steve Collett) 10 divers, 31ft, all electronic gear. Tel: (0329) 220461.

At Portsmouth: *Woodpecker* (Skippers Paul and Dave Faithfull) 12 divers; 33ft, all electronic gear. Tel: (0705) 833923.

At Langstone: *Griffin* (Skippers Ike Curran and Frank Walker) 12 divers, 50ft, all electronic gear. Tel: (0252) 330941.

Area 5: Culver Cliff to St. Catherine's Point

This section runs south from 50 40 00 to the edge of Chart No. 2045. The area is bounded in the east by 00 56 00 and runs west to 01 17 00. This means that it encompasses much of the best of Isle of Wight diving, which means boat diving.

The tides here are less complicated than elsewhere, but just as strong. The flood tide runs to the east in the area south of St. Catherine's Point and slowly turns to the north-east following the shape of the Island's coastline. The strongest streams run south of St. Catherine's Point and between St. Catherine's and Dunnose Point. Off St. Catherine's the flood tide can reach a speed of four-and-a-half knots and four knots on the ebb. The strength of these streams reduces the further you go out from the Island. Slack water periods occur at about one hour before and four-and-a-half to five hours after High Water Portsmouth. Inshore of Sandown Bay the streams turn earlier, with the ebb turning between two and three hours before High Water Portsmouth.

This area is very much holidaymaker territory on land and in season the visiting diver should make allowances for slow traffic between resorts.

Niton. Every dive boat and every ship fitted with radio operating for miles along the Channel coast will know this call-sign. The famous Niton Radio Station is just 800 yards east-north-east of St. Catherine's Point. The huge radio masts are an easy landmark.

Launch sites
Yaverland. This launch site is off Yaverland Road and the B3395. Here there is a good concrete ramp beside the Yaverland Sailing and Boating Club. The ramp is fairly steep and runs at an angle to the sandy beach. There is a large car park nearby.

Sandown. A large ramp runs on to the sandy beach at the end of the Esplanade. Approach by Pier Street, off the High Street. Parking nearby is limited.

Shanklin. There is a large ramp at the end of the Esplanade on to the sandy beach with a car park close by. Another ramp is available by Shanklin Sailing Club, off Hope Road. There is a small car park alongside.

Shore diving sites
134 Sandown. This is a popular resort lying in the centre of Sandown Bay. The 400 yard pier, which runs south-east from the shore, is very popular with visitors and divers. Acess is straightforward from the beach, but trying to park close by can be a real problem in the busy tourist season. The

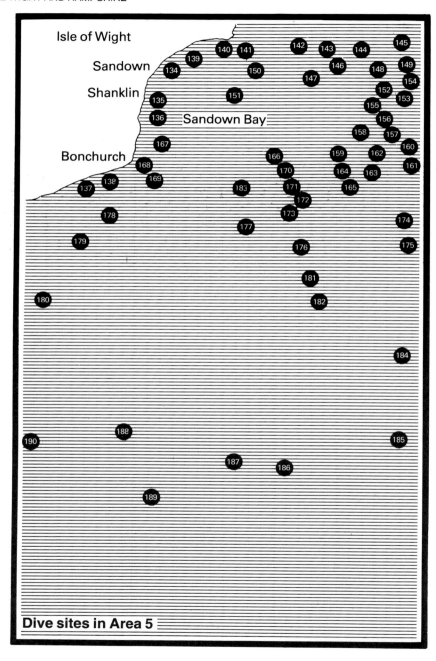

Dive sites in Area 5

seabed here is mostly sand, but there are a few rocky gullies towards the pier head. Maximum depth is about 7m at High Water.

135 Shanklin. Another very popular resort, lying one and threequarter miles north of Dunnose. It too has a pier, with a prominent white tower at the shore end and a pavilion at its head. The seabed is sandy, but there are more rock gullies than at Sandown. Depth is 7m maximum.

136 The Moorings. This is a small outcrop of rocks, just to the south of the head of Shanklin Pier. It is so called because it provides good holding ground for small boat anchors. The area is shallow with a maximum depth of 7m. Shallow but interesting, for all sorts of items have been found by local divers including an all-brass antique outboard! Crabs and lobsters can be included among those interesting items too!

137 Ventnor. This seaside resort has a population of some 7,000 in winter and it doubles when the tourists flock in. It lies in a sheltered position under St. Boniface Down which is the highest point on the Island at 236m. The pier at Ventnor is currently in a poor state after a fire in 1986 and much of it is closed to the public. Diving is quite interesting, with easy access off the beach and a rocky seabed with gullies over two metres deep. Close to the east of the pier head is The Bean, a rock which dries over 2m at Low Springs. There are obstructions around the rock and bits of old wreckage.

138 Chancellor. This old paddlesteamer was wrecked by the pier at Ventnor in 1863. Parts of her can still be found on the northern side of the pier in very shallow water less than 10m, but she is very, very broken.

Boat diving sites:

139 Hauler. At 50 38 54; 01 08 33. Depth: 14m. The *Hauler* was a 100-foot-long crane barge used by harbour contractors for piling and dredging operations. She had no propulsion of her own. On September 18, 1973 she was being towed across Sandown Bay when the tow parted. Before it could be re-connected, she had taken on a lot of water and started sinking, finally going to the bottom just half a mile to the east of Sandown Pier.

For two years the site was marked with a wreck buoy until September 1975 when a certain amount of salvage was carried out. Finally in October 1976 the barge was dispersed with explosives.

Today this wreck is very flat and the highest part, some hull plates, stand no more than 1½ metres off the seabed, which is mainly mud with a covering of fine sand. Amongst the wreckage are yards of rusting wire hawsers and parts of winches. There is no evidence of the actual crane itself and this may lie some distance from the main wreckage. Either side of the wreck are several large wooden piles of approximately 12" square, probably being carried on the barge. The wreck lies east and west.

About 50 yards to the north-east of the site is a good sized rocky outcrop which stands several metres off the bottom. This is often picked up on echo sounders and mistaken for the wreck of the *Hauler*.

Bembridge 5.5 miles; Portsmouth 10.5 miles.

140 Harry Sharman. At 50 39 48; 01 06 14. Depth: 5m. In November 1970 a collision between the 42,000-ton crude-oil carriers *Pacific Glory* and the 46,000-ton *Allegro* left the former crippled and burning at the stern. The old

The tug Harry Sharman *was sent to assist in pollution control after the collision between oil-carriers* Allegro *and* Pacific Glory *in 1970. She ended up stranded.*

steam tug *Harry Sharman* was sent out to assist with oil pollution control. During this work the tug broke down and ended up stranding at the base of Culver Cliff immediately below the Yarborough Monument. Attempts to salvage were unsuccessful and the tug was left to the elements. She is easy to find especially at Low Water when parts of her boiler stick above the surface. Care is needed as much of the wreck is only just below the surface and could easily be hit by a small boat. Most of the superstructure and the decking have collapsed. The hull is still recognisable and her steel propeller is in place.

This is a good shallow or second dive. Small boats can be launched from the beach at Yaverland just a mile away.

Bembridge 3.5 miles; Portsmouth 8.5 miles.

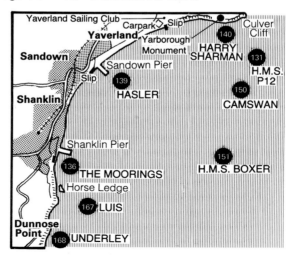

Cut in two in a collision, the Patrol Boat P12 was one of a class used for escort duty and as submarine hunters.

141 H.M.S. P-12. At 50 39 24; 01 05 00. Depth: 22m. H.M. Patrol Boat *P-12* was part of the Portsmouth escort force during WW1. On November 4, 1918, she was on patrol off the Isle of Wight, when she was in collision with another vessel, which cut her in two. The larger stern section sank in the given position, just half-a-mile to the south east of Culver Cliff. The bow section was eventually beached in Whitecliff Bay. *The Times* of November 7, 1918 reported one man missing, believed drowned in the collision.

The stern section is a recently discovered wreck. It was found in 1985 by a small team of divers led by Martin Pritchard.

These patrol boats were designed early in the war primarily to help relieve destroyers of escort duty, and to be effective submarine hunters. Some 45 P-Boats were built under an emergency programme during 1915-17 and proved to be very successful.

The dimensions of these boats were 244ft x 23ft x 7ft. The 613-ton boats were powered by twin steam turbines providing 3,500h.p., which gave a top speed of 20 knots.

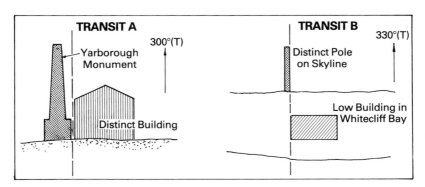

Relics of the P12, which was discovered by a group lead by Martin Pritchard, include steam gauges, two cabin oil lamps, three portholes and a complete Walker trailing log.

The P.12 was built by J.S. White's of Cowes, Isle of Wight and launched on December 4, 1915. She went into service in February, 1916.

The wreck is an interesting dive. The stern sank on to a fairly firm seabed and sits upright. It is fairly intact and the sharply cut-down counter and larger rudder are quite plain. On the stern deck are many old and now harmless depth charges still in their racks. Further forward the depth charge throwing arms are cocked back and loaded waiting for a U-Boat to appear. Finning further forward will bring you to the large turbines.

First dives on this one were a wreck diver's dream! Portholes were lying at regular spaces along the hull having fallen out of the rotting steel hull. Around the engines row after row of steam gauges with their needles still set at their working pressure were found, along with many other interesting artifacts. The wreckage is long and narrow and lies across the tide in a north-west – south-east direction, with the stern to the north-west.

Part of the bow section is sometimes uncovered on the beach at 50 40 15; 01 05 30. (See Site 131).

Bembridge 3.5 miles; Portsmouth 8.5 miles.

142 Obstruction. At 50 39 50; 01 02 13. Depth: 13m. An obstruction is in this position on the south-eastern edge of the Princessa Shoal, 2 miles east of Culver Cliff. It is very small and stands just half a metre high. No other information is available.

Bembridge 3 miles; Portsmouth 8 miles.

143 New Venture. At 50 39 18; 01 01 42. Depth: 20m. The *New Venture* was a 42ft fishing boat which sank on December 31, 1978 in this approximate position, 3 miles east of Yarborough Monument. No diving information is available.

144 Unknown. At 50 39 16; 00 59 03. Depth: 21m. This unkown wreck lies 4 miles to the east of Culver Cliffs. However the wreckage may be only part of a ship as the site is fairly small.

She was dived in 1964 and the divers described the wreck as around 80ft long and 25ft wide. She was a steel-hulled vessel of double bottom construction. There was considerable wreckage extending some forty yards from the main section.

Subsequent dives have showed that the steelwork is of fairly light construction and that the largest part of the wreck is some form of steel tank which is also the highest part, standing just 1½m high. There is no sign of any propulsion, which could indicate that a part of the ship is missing, but is is quite likely that this is a fuel or water barge that was being towed across the Channel during Operation Neptune in June 1944. On a recent dive a dinner plate was recovered from the site which had the inscription – "Southampton Masonic . . . Co" on it. Is this a clue?

The site is of small extent and is not easy to locate. Most of the scattered wreckage appears now to be buried into the sand and gravel seabed.

Bembridge 5 miles; Portsmouth 9.5 miles.

145 Obstruction. At 50 39 59; 00 57 28. Depth: 15m. A small obstruction was located just a quarter of a mile south-west of the Nab Tower during a 1978 survey. No other information available.

Bembridge 5.5 miles; Portsmouth 10 miles.

146 Unknown. 50 39 12; 01 01 10. Depth: 20m. This wreck was first located in the early 1970's, and was at first believed to be the British collier *Stanwold,* but that wreck has been identified and located in position 50 38 00N;00 20 02 W in Sussex waters. This one is 3 miles east of Culver Cliff and was first dived in 1978. The divers reported finding a very broken and generally flat wreck, with isolated peaks of around 2m. The bows were to the east-north-east and the stern to the south-west complete with iron propeller.

Dived again in 1986, the wreck was confirmed as very flat with plates and ribs standing only inches off the seabed. One larger section was seen, approximately 5 metres square and stood 2½ metres off the bottom, probably part of the bow. Very little was recognisable and the stern was not seen. On later dives, bottles and jars found here were of British origin. Plenty of coal lying around would indicate that it was a steamship, or she was a collier but no boiler has been seen so far.

Bembridge 4 miles; Portsmouth 9 miles.

147 Estrelita. At 50 38 50; 01 01 54. Depth: 25m. This is a 25-ton 50ft wooden MFV and stands 2m proud. She was sunk on August 3, 1975 and is now very broken.

Bembridge 4 miles; Portsmouth 9 miles.

148 Unknown. At 50 38 33; 00 59 10. Depth: 17m. This "wreckage", two miles south-west of the Nab Tower, was first located in 1978. It was about 100ft long and 50ft wide standing 2-4m high and lying east and west. This position has twice been surveyed since then with a proton magnetometer, but no firm contacts were picked up. The only real contact was on the echo sounder which did pick up an obstruction of similar proportions, but this appeared to be a rocky outcrop. The dimensions given earlier do not sound shipshape, and diving on the site confirmed the presence of a rocky outcrop. This is now called "Crab Rocks" locally as it is a good spot for edible crabs. Divers have found some small brass fittings among the rocks but nothing to justify calling this a wreck site.

Bembridge 5 miles; Portsmouth 10 miles.

149 Unknown. At 50 38 39; 00 58 24. Depth: 18m. This site was first located in 1974 1¾ miles south-west of the Nab Tower, and was believed to have been a small fishing boat. The site has since been dived by Portsmouth diver Mike Walsh who found a most unusual "wreck". It is a large box section made up of several compartments. It is around 40ft long, and 12ft wide and stands two metres high. There is a bulkhead between each compartment and a large hole through each one in the same position.

The wreckage lies in an east-west direction and is part of the harbour sections being towed to France on D-Day.

150 Camswan. At 50 38 42; 01 05 23. Depth: 18m. The 3426-ton British steamship *Camswan* was built in 1917 by the Blyth Shipbuilding Company of steel with corrugated sides. She measured 335ft x 51ft x 23ft. She was fitted with a triple expansion steam engine of 298h.p.

At the time of her loss she was owned by the Osborne Steamship Company of Blyth. On October 19, 1917, on her maiden voyage from Blyth to Naples with a cargo of coal, she was in collision with another British Steamship the *Polbrai* eight miles south-west of St. Catherine's Point. The *Camswan* was badly damaged but managed to make it into the shallow waters of Sandown Bay before sinking 1½ miles south-east of Culver cliff. All her crew were saved.

Large parts of the wreck were dispersed with explosives during the 1920's, but this is a large site with plenty to explore. Average height of the wreckage is 3-4m. The ship's sternpost stands defiantly about 4m high, with her large steel propeller behind it. Some parts of the wreck are completely flat but she is still a good rummage dive, as Island diver John Nuttall will testify. In 1989 John found one of the ship's smaller bells in a newly-collapsed section of the wreck. It was engraved "S.S. CAMSWAN 1917". Shortly afterwards Martin Woodward found her telegraph.

151 HMS Boxer. at 50 37 46; 01 06 22. Depth: 20m. *HMS Boxer* was one of

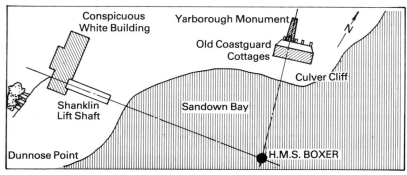

Marks for HMS Boxer. (Site 151).

Completed in 1895, HMS Boxer *was one of Britain's earliest destroyers. She suffered two collisions in three days and sank in 1918. Courtesy Marine Photo Library, Cromer.*

Britain's earliest destroyers. One of three identical ships, she was the first of the 'A' class torpedo boat destroyers. The other two ships were *HMS Ardent* and *HMS Bruiser. Boxer* was 200ft long with a beam of 19ft. She was laid down in February 1894 and finally completed in June 1895 by Thornycroft at their Chiswick yard. During her three-hour trial she achieved a top speed of 29.17 knots. Her estimated cost of building was £35,780. She carried a crew of 55. The *Boxer* was armed with one 12pdr and five 6pdr guns and two 14" torpedo tubes. Her triple expansion engines drove two shafts and produced some 4,000h.p. giving her a speed of 27 knots. For fuel she carried 60 tons of coal.

At the time of her loss the 260-ton *Boxer* was Britain's oldest serving destroyer, but maybe her luck was starting to run out. On February 6, 1918, she was in collision with *HMS Decoy,* then two days later on February 8, she collided with the ambulance transport ship *St Patrick* 1½ miles south-east of Dunnose Point, just after 7 o'clock in the evening. The *Boxer* was badly damaged, one man was killed and she was slowly sinking. She finally went down in the centre of Sandown Bay at 0015 hrs on February 9. Her commanding officer, Lt-Cmdr J.K. Chaplin was court-martialled but the records are closed to the public until 1993.

The wreck site lies 2½ miles out from the beach at Sandown. She was first dived in the early 1970's by the Deo Volente Club, who tried unsuccessfully to purchase her. During 1972 a salvage company raised the condensers and props. In the years following she became a popular dive for members of the Shanklin Underwater Club. They recovered many interesting items, including some rum jars. One diver, Dougie Saunders, was lucky – his jar was still full and well corked!

Today the wreck has largely disappeared. Very little of the hull remains. Only her boilers stand some 3m off the mud and sand seabed but bits and pieces are still found by those willing to dig into the mud.

Bembridge 5 miles; Portsmouth 10 miles.

152 Unknown. At 50 38 07; 00 59 32. Depth: 20m. A small double obstruction is located in this position 2½ miles south-west of the Nab Tower. It was reported to be only 0.6m high. No diving information available.
Bembridge 5½ miles; Portsmouth 10 miles.

153 Elford. At 50 38 08; 00 58 29. Depth: 24m. The 1739-ton steamer *Elford* ran into a mine laid by a U-boat two miles south of the Nab Light Vessel on May 18, 1917. All her crew managed to take to the boats safely before she sank. The wreck was believed to have broken up some years ago and so she was deleted from the charts. In fact, much of the ship remains though most of the hull has rusted away. She is well broken but her boiler, engine and steering quadrant still stand some 5-6m proud. Within the wreck, which is still recognisable as a ship, are many railway wheels and bogies which were part of her cargo. The bow points to the west. The stern section is lying over some 40 degrees on her starboard side. She is difficult to locate as she lies amid an isolated area of rocks which stand almost as proud as she does.
Bembridge 6 miles; Portsmouth 11½ miles.

154 Steel Barge. At 50 38 32; 00 56 21. Depth: 20m. This is a steel barge, 2 miles south of the Nab Tower. She is around 60ft long, lies east and west, and stands 3m high. The barge is motorised as two engines and drives have been seen. She is fairly intact and sits upright. Her hold is completely filled with a large cylindrical container.
This wreck is very similar to Site 144 and was probably another fuel or water barge heading for the Normandy beaches during Operation Neptune in June 1944.
Bembridge 7 miles; Portsmouth 11 miles.

155 The Hump. at 50 38 00; 00 58 44. Depth: 20m. A large mound giving a strong magnetic anomaly is located in this position 2 miles south-west of the Nab Tower. The site has been dived, but no wreckage was found. Whatever it is, appears to be completely buried in the seabed of sand and shingle.
Bembridge 6 miles, Portsmouth 11.5 miles.

156 HMT Apley. At 50 36 59; 00 56 00. Depth: 35m. This Royal navy hired trawler was sunk by a mine on December 6, 1917 while engaged in sweeping duties. A 250-ton ship, she is now upright six metres proud on the seabed of shingle. The mine explosion has caused a great deal of damage to her bow and she lies east-west.
Bembridge 7½ miles; Portsmouth 12 miles.

157 Barge. At 50 37 00; 00 58 30. Depth: 28m. A small wreck of barge shape about 50ft long with a beam of 24ft, lies north to south on the edge of a steep slope, from which she stands five metres proud.
Bembridge 6½ miles; Portsmouth 11½ miles.

158 Unknown. At 50 38 31; 00 59 00. Depth: 18m. Guarded on the north by a rocky ridge 100 yards from the actual wreck site, this is a tricky one to find. The wreck appears to be only 30ft long, but it is impossible to tell this accurately from sonar details as the wreck lies down the slope of a steep bank. Diving information required.
Bembridge 5½ miles; Portsmouth 10 miles.

159 Pontoons. At 50 36 22; 01 00 55. Depth: 25m. This site consists of two large steel pontoons. Each one measures about 145ft by 32ft. They are 10 yards apart, joined together by some sort of steel mesh, and lie east to west with a maximum height of 3m. These may well have been two of the many harbour and bridge sections that were designed to be towed across the Channel to Normandy during, operation Neptune in June 1944.

Bembridge 6.5 miles; Portsmouth 11.5 miles.

160 Bettan (bow). At 50 36 08; 00 57 20. Depth: 40m. This wreck is the bow section of the Danish motor vessel *Bettan* which sank off St. Helen's on January 19, 1967 (see Site 126 for details of loss and stern section).

The bow section was towed out to the deep water spoil ground six miles south-east of Culver Cliff and sunk there.

The site was dived in 1976 and the divers reported finding the bow half of a fairly modern ship, about 25m long and standing eight metres high. There was a diesel engine mounted on the foredeck. They also said that the hold appeared to be full of clay. This would certainly tie in with the *Bettann* as she was carrying a cargo of china clay at the time of her loss. The wreck lies across the tide in a north-east and south-west direction.

Bembridge 8 miles; Portsmouth 13 miles.

161 Unknown. At 50 36 02; 00 56 28. Depth: 43m. This site is of a very small wreck. She is just 25ft long and stands less than 2m off the bottom which is mainly sand. It may be that this is a small fishing boat or just a part of a wreck, but is more likely to be discarded debris of some sort as this spot is right in the centre of the deep water spoil ground six miles south-east of Culver Cliff.

Bembridge 8 miles; Portsmouth 13 miles.

162 Cuba. At 50 36 00; 00 58 35. Depth: 32m. This is the largest wreck in the area. She was a very big kill for Kapitanleutnant Ernst Cordes on April 6, 1945, so big in fact that it brought about his own destruction and that of his submarine *U-1195*.

The story of the *Cuba* starts when she was built as a two-funnel

Two-funnel passenger liner Cuba, *built in 1923 and torpedoed and sunk in 1945. Her complement of over 250 men was able to escape as she settled slowly in an upright position.*

passenger liner for the French Cie Générale Transatlantique by Swan Hunter and Wigham Richardson of Newcastle in 1923. She was 476ft long with a beam of 62ft and her 10,300h.p. engines could push her 11,420 tons along at 15.5 knots. She was designed by the French company for the West Indies and Central American run. Her peacetime cruising career came to an abrupt end after she left Martinique on October 24, 1940 bound for Casablanca, but was intercepted by a British warship on October 31. After that she sailed under the British flag and was used sometimes as a troopship. She was managed for the Ministry of War Transport by Cunard White Star.

She was acting as a trooper when she was heading home to Southampton from Le Havre with 223 troops and crew aboard, plus 29 gunners for her many guns, as part of Convoy VWP 16 on April 6, 1945. This convoy had six destroyers as escorts, but when Ernst Cordes saw her through his periscope he just could not let her pass. At exactly 04.13 he hit her fair and square with one torpedo. That torpedo only killed one crewman but it did the necessary damage to sink her. As *U-1195* turned away the *Cuba* began to settle slowly and stayed upright to the end. This enabled all aboard to be taken off before she went under.

The destroyers were after Cordes from the moment the torpedo struck. And they hunted him down. He and his crew of 34 were depth-charged out of existence before he had gone three miles from the grave of the *Cuba*. The actual killed was made by *HMS Watchman*, whose depth charges blew the U-boat in two. (See Site 175).

The *Cuba* has been heavily salvaged over the years and was dispersed by the Royal Navy in 1959. The majority of the ship is well-broken, but some parts of the wreckage still stand 14m proud. This is a fascinating dive with wreckage all around. Some areas are quite recognisable though much of it seems to be piles of steel plate and great girders. It is a very large site and will need several dives to see most of it. The *Cuba* was a luxury liner in her day and her passengers had hundreds of portholes to look out of on their voyages. There were actually in excess of 200 portholes on her and many of them are still hidden among the wreckage, which has a scour nearly 2m deep on the north-east side. The wreckage lies north-east to south-west on a seabed of mud, shingle and sand which is deeply rippled. Visibility is usually poor from dumping on the close-by spoil ground. Both her 10-ton propellors have been salvaged.

Bembridge 8 miles; Portsmouth 12 miles.

163 Unknown. At 50 35 42; 00 58 32. Depth: 30m. A difficult one to spot on the ordinary echo-sounder, due to the fact that the seabed consists of rocky ridges with sand valleys, but this 42ft "unknown" is definitely there. Well broken, she is lying east to west and standing 4m proud in an area of particularly steep ridging.

Bembridge 8 miles; Portsmouth 12.5 miles.

164 Piper Aircraft G-ARLS. At 50 35 58; 01 00 40. Depth: 30m. This *Piper* light aircraft ditched into the sea 4½ miles south-west of the Nab Tower on July 31, 1975 after losing power in both engines. The pilot escaped with minor injuries. The area was surveyed a month later and an obstruction standing some 2m off the seabed was located. More recently a local fisherman is said to have got his pot lines hooked into a plane in this area and managed to winch the whole thing off the bottom before it broke away.

If it was the Piper then it may well be in a new position nearby.
Bembridge 6.5 miles; Portsmouth 11.5 miles.

165 Spoil Ground Wreck. At 50 35 51; 00 59 24. Depth 35m. Whether this is in fact a wreck it is difficult to say. Either way she or it has never been dived and was located by magnetometer only. Whatever it is sits in the middle of spoil ground where salvage divers say there are bits of metal, large and small, all over the place. As a result of the doubt over the wreck's existence, the Admiralty do not chart it or her.
Bembridge 8 miles; Portsmouth 13 miles.

166 Leon. At 50 35 42; 01 03 40. Depth: 30m. This wreck lies 4.5 miles east of Dunnose Point and is not marked on the charts.

To say that Captain Louis Orchambeau was asking for it is, perhaps, too strong. But he certainly was careless for he went down Channel as dawn was breaking – on January 7, 1918 – with all his navigation lights on and he did not even bother to zig-zag his 2451-ton steamer *Leon*. Oberleutnant Johann Lohs, captain of the mine-laying U-boat *UC-75* could hardly believe his eyes. Ignoring the fact that the French collier *Leon* was clearly armed with two big 90mm cannon, he surfaced to make his torpedo shot all the easier.

By now it was dawn, the weather was moderate with an overcast sky and visibility at about one mile. The *Leon* came on across the submarine's bow at a steady seven knots, steering a course west by north magnetic. Captain Orchambeau and a lookout were on the bridge. Another lookout was on the forecastle. But, incredibly, none of them saw *UC-75*. They felt her all right.

At 5a.m. Lohs' torpedo struck her in the starboard side and blew a great hole into No. 2 hold. *UC-75* had submerged as soon as she had let go the torpedo and the crew of the *Leon* were convinced that they had struck a mine. They believed that until metal fragments they picked up from her deck were later examined by the Commanding Officer of H.M. Mining School and identified as pieces of a German torpedo.

Lohs had no doubt that he had hit her and hung around watching through his periscope until she sank 75 minutes after the torpedo struck. He then turned for home and re-entered Zeebrugge on January 8.

On board the *Leon* there was a small panic among the 34 crew. Four of them ignored the Master's orders and rushed to launch one of the small lifeboats. They made the fatal mistake of lowering it into the water before the ship had lost way and as it hit the water it capsized. The four men were never seen again. If Lohs had feared that the *Leon*'s wireless would bring depth-charging patrol boats down on him, he need not have worried. Captain Orchambeau quickly found that the explosion had put his radio completely out of action. He waited for a while until it was clear that the *Leon* was sinking under them and then ordered "abandon ship". This time all of the rest of the crew got into the lifeboats without difficulty and were able to sit in the boats and watch their ship take her final plunge to the seabed. Eventually the survivors of the *Leon* were picked up by a patrol boat and landed safely on the Isle of Wight.

Today the *Leon* is well broken up midships, and heeled over to starboard. In place on the stern is a large gun. The bows are badly damaged but stand high at around 8m. The site does appear to have had some salvage work carried out. In the wreckage are numbers of small stone jars, still corked and full of blue ink.

Bembridge 7.5 miles; Portsmouth 12.5 miles.

167 Luis. At 50 36 27; 01 09 55. Depth: 17m. This site is the wreck of the British merchant steamship *Luis*. She was built in 1916 of steel by W. Gray and Company of West Hartlepool. She measured 380ft x 53ft x 24ft. At the time of her loss she was owned by C. Nielson and Sons.

The 2484-ton *Luis* had left Halifax Harbour, Nova Scotia, Canada with a cargo of flour, oats, timber and many tons of 18lb anti-personnel artillery shells destined for the battlefields of France. On April 12, 1918, while rounding St. Catherine's Point in a 20-ship convoy, she was torpedoed by the German submarine *UC-71*. Oberleutnant Marzecha attacked the convoy in the dark of the evening, despite its strong escort, from a surface position.

Captain P.W. Woodruff was able to coax his sinking ship in towards the shallow water of Sandown Bay where she finally sank just a quarter of a mile offshore opposite Luccombe Chine. Four seamen lost their lives.

For many years after she sank her masts funnel and bridge were clearly

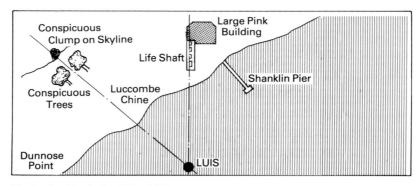

Marks for the Luis. (Site 167).

visible sticking out of the water. When these finally collapsed in 1921, the Navy decided that the wreck should be dispersed, as she was a danger to other ships being only just below the surface. Dispersal blasting operations were completed in 1923.

The *Luis* was forgotten until the early 1970's when a salvage team located the wreck and began hauling up the many tons of shells. People on the beach were entranced to see the crewmen on the salvage vessel breaking the shells from their boxes and then smashing them across the ship's bollards to separate the heads from the brass cases!

Today the *Luis* is a popular dive site. There is plenty to explore. The wreck is well broken up, but her two huge boilers and parts of the stern stand some 3-4m off the seabed. On the north side of the boilers, it is still possible to find the odd shell case and the intricate brass shell heads that the salvage men left behind. Scattered all around the site are hundreds of small round lead shot from the anti-personnel filling of the large shells.

The tidal stream runs quite hard especially on the ebb. Slack water times on the Luis are 3-2½ hours before High Water Portsmouth and 5 hours after.

Small boats can be launched from Shanklin beach, which is only a mile from the site.

Bembridge 7 miles; Portsmouth 12 miles.

168 Underley. At 50 36 00; 01 11 00. Depth 3m. It was very dark but calm on the night of September 25, 1871. Even so the fully-rigged sailing ship *Underley* ran on to rocks just offshore between Bonchurch and Luccombe on the Island. She was a fine ship, 225ft long with a beam of 37ft and listed as 1292 tons.

The *Underley* was heading for Melbourne, Australia with a cargo of machinery, gunpowder and cotton worth some £30,000. In addition she carried 30 emigrating passengers.

It was expected that the ship would be quickly towed off after she went ashore, but a fresh wind sprang up from the south-east and impaled the ship on the rocks. At that time she was the largest sailing ship to become a total loss. The passengers and crew were soon taken ashore and the *Underley* was abandoned where she lay.

Today the wreck is almost totally broken up, but if you dive around the rocks you can find parts of her scattered there. Larger bits have become buried in the sand. The site is worth visiting after a strong south-easterly gale as this can remove large quantities of sand from the site and expose many new parts of the wreck.

Although the site is very close to the shore, the tide can run quite quickly here and rummagers should take care not to be caught.

Bembridge 8 miles; Portsmouth 13.5 miles.

169 Unknown. At 50 35 20; 01 10.09. Depth: 50m. An unknown obstruction was reported in this position in 1980. At one time this was believed to be the wreck of the *Polo*, but *Polo* has now been confirmed by her bell as Site 170.

170 Polo. At 50 35 36; 01 03 59. Depth: 30m. Oberleutnant Johann Lohs torpedoed this British ship from *UB-57* just as dusk was falling on February

This fine three-master, the Underley, *on the way to Australia with cargo and emigrants, ran onto offshore rocks between Bonchurch and Luccombe in 1871. Courtesy of Tom Rayner.*

12, 1918. The 2915-ton *Polo,* 300ft long with a beam of 45ft, is described as a liner, but that did not refer to her size but to the fact that she carried passengers as well as cargo. She was built in 1913 by Earles of Hull.

It is doubtful if the lookouts on the *Polo* saw anything of Lohs as he fired one torpedo from periscope depth at her as she came down Channel on a voyage from Hull to Malta and Alexandria. Three men died in the sinking which was very swift. Her cargo was described as coal and general Government supplies, but Lohs had no doubt about what she carried. He wrote in his log: "In Admiralty service with a cargo of mines for the Mediterranean." Obviously divers should bear this in mind when diving her! Her bell has been recovered. The stern section appears broken and heeled to port. A large steering quadrant stands proud. The stern appears to be the highest part, standing up to 7m off the bottom. Cabin oil lamps have been recovered.

If Lohs had feared that the *Leon* wireless would bring depth-charging patrol boats down on him, he need not have worried. Captain Orchambeau quickly found that the explosion had put his radio completely out of action. He waited for a while until it was clear that the *Leon* was sinking under them and then ordered "abandon ship". This time all of the rest of the crew got into the lifeboats without difficulty and were able to sit in the boats and watch their ship take her final plunge to the seabed.

The *Leon* was located by salvage divers in 1975. She lies north-south and was upright, standing 10m proud. More recent diving shows that the wreck has broken up a great deal since first found, possibly due to salvage work on her and her cargo of 2250 tons of coal and 600 tons of coke, which she was taking from the Tyne to Tunis. The bow area now seems much flattened and the starboard side has collapsed leaving the deck at a steep angle. The highest point now is the boiler which stands some 4m off the bottom of the wreckage. Two portholes were recovered on a recent dive.

Bembridge 7 miles; Portsmouth 12 miles.

171 Unknown. At 50 35 05; 01 02 36. Depth: 30m. This unknown was first located in 1983 by sonar.

This site was dived in 1986, and is a steel wreck, fairly small around 60ft long, and broken in two midships. The bow section is totally upside down. The stern lies on its port side and there is a three-bladed steel propeller of about 2m diameter partially buried in the bottom. Alongside the wreck are two steel masts of about 20cm diameter. This gives the impression that the wreck is of an old trawler. There seems to be an abundance of marine life on this site including giant crabs! The wreck stands a maximum of 3m off the shingle and sand seabed.

Bembridge 7 miles; Portsmouth 12 miles.

172 Unknown. 50 34 44; 01 03 20. Depth: 35m. This unknown wreck was first reported in February 1918, when a passing ship saw a mast sticking out of the water five miles east of Dunnose Point. The wreck today is still unidentified but she is certainly a good-sized merchant steamship. She sits upright and lies roughly north-west and south-east. She is around 300ft long and stands 6-7m off the bottom, which is mainly stone and shingle. She is badly damaged around her midships section probably from either a mine or torpedo. She has four holds and her cargo appears to have been mainly bricks. Her large single iron propeller is still in place.

Bembridge 8 miles; Portsmouth 13 miles.

173 Coaster. At 50 34 28; 01 03 34. Depth: 30m. This is the wreck of an old coaster of World War One vintage. Dived in 1989, she is upright, iron propeller in place, and a gun on the aft deck. A shell case for the gun is of 75mm calibre, indicating a French gun, and possibly a French ship. Her cargo is varied but much appears to be cases of .303 rifles. Bows are broken and deeper at 35m. Boiler is highest point at 7m.

Bembridge 8 miles; Portsmouth 13 miles.

174 Tenace. At 50 34 36; 00 56 03. Depth: 30m. The 23-ton yacht *Tenace* sank in this position, 5½ miles south of the Nab Tower, after being in collision with the Japanese motor vessel *Heian Maru* on July 14, 1967. The position was surveyed in 1977, but since then no evidence of the wreck has been found and it is believed to have broken up completely.

Bembridge 9.5 miles; Portsmouth 15 miles.

175 U-1195. At 50 33 17; 00 56 09. Depth: 30m. Kapitanleutnant Ernst Cordes and his crew of 34 were all killed on April 6, 1945 after his attack on Convoy No. VWP 16 as it headed for Southampton across Sandown Bay towards the Solent (See Site 162). The convoy had six destroyers as escorts and they all turned on him after he torpedoed the trooper *Cuba*. Cordes ran to the south-east and the deeper water, but the destroyers were too quickly on his trail to let him escape. So he sat his Mark VII U-boat on the seabed and shut down all machinery. The ruse did not work and the escorts were soon overhead. They pounded the seabed all around Cordes's suspected position. For the record it was a depth-charge from *HMS Watchman*, which landed right beside the 871-ton 220ft long submarine, blew in the hull near the conning tower, and sent all the crew to Kingdom Come.

It was a swift end to a short career as a U-boat captain for Ernst Cordes. He first appears in records as a U-boat commander on July 5, 1944, when from *U-763* he sent a torpedo with a pre-set gyro and a zig-zag course right into the side of the 1499-ton Norwegian steamer *Ringen* at precisely 1603 hours that afternoon. The *Ringen* was an old ship – built in 1917 with her home port Oslo – but was being used in Convoy ETC 26 on the eastern feeder route to supply the Allied armies in Normandy. She sank swiftly. But Cordes was not satisfied on his command debut with just one ship. That same day at 2145 he damaged another steamer of 4,000-tons with an acoustic homing torpedo called a "Gnat". Three minutes later another of his torpedoes exploded on a 3,000-ton steamer. At 2200 he claimed another strike.

Ernst Cordes was no different from other U-boat captains of WW2. They were prone to classify all torpedo detonations as hits despite the fact that torpedoes often exploded for other reasons, such as the tendency of acoustic torpedoes to explode in ships' wakes.

It was a fact too, that U-boats attacking convoys in groups often calculated their hits on the number of explosions seen or heard and their claims were often duplicated in this way.

However, there is no doubt that Ernst Cordes may have come into command late in the war but he had made an impressive debut. He appears again, still in command of *U-763*, on July 11 when he claimed to have sunk a destroyer with a Gnat torpedo, but there is no record of any British warship being sunk on that date. Certainly Cordes made an attack and reported hearing one Gnat end-of-run detonation after nine minutes and 28 seconds and may well have confused this with a hit.

He next appears in German records – and goes straight into many a diver's logbook – when, on March 21, 1945, now commanding *U-1195* he sank the much-dived Liberty ship James Eagan Layne. It was on that same mission, though now much further up the Channel, that he sank the *Cuba* on April 6, and brought destruction on himself.

Although an approximate position was known for *U-1195* ever since her sinking, it was not until 1975 that a salvage company finally pinned down the exact spot.

Today the submarine lies on her starboard side at an angle of 45 degrees. She lies on a slight sand-shingle slope with her bows to the north-east and down the slope. There is very severe damage – from the depth-charge – just forward of the conning tower. The stern is high and both steel propellers are still there and well clear of the bottom. The wreck – 200ft long with a beam of 20ft and a depth of 16ft – stands some four metres proud of the seabed.

The highest point is the top of her periscope in which the optical lens can still be seen. The deck gun is missing. The damaged area in front of the conning tower has made a hole large enough to swim into. Though the bulkhead is still intact, the watertight door is missing and you can see straight into the control room through the metre-wide opening. This part is heavily silted. So much so that the lower parts of the periscopes go on down into the silt. Her torpedo tubes are still in place and are of steel. The pressure hull is rotting and holes are appearing in it. Through one of these you can see one of her large air tanks. The visibility around her is usually good, due to light being reflected upwards off the pale coloured sand and shingle of the bottom.

Bembridge 11 miles; Portsmouth 16 miles.

176 Unknown. At 50 33 15; 01 03 37. Depth: 31m. This unknown was first located in 1918. She lies 5 miles east of Ventnor. Her existence was again confirmed during a 1961 survey.

The wreck was first dived by salvage divers in 1975 and they reported finding an old coaster, standing some 5m proud of the sand and gravel seabed. She was dived again in 1986. The remains are now very broken and mostly unrecognisable. It is likely that this is a WW1 wreck. The bows are fairly intact, and a large anchor with masses of chain was mixed up within the wreckage. The wreck appears well salvaged, as there are many old hawsers, 45-gallon drums and old tyres spread around the site.

Bembridge 9 miles; Portsmouth 14 miles.

177 Unknown. At 50 34 10; 01 05 50. Depth: 20m. An unknown ship was reported sunk in this approximate position 3½ miles east of Dunnose Point in May 1918 when two masts were seen sticking out of the water.

Bembridge 9 miles; Portsmouth 14 miles.

178 S.M.S. Baden. In St. Catherine's Deep. Depth: 60m. The *SMS Baden* was a large German battle-cruiser, which was handed over to Britain at the end of WW1. She was towed out of Portsmouth Harbour to be used as a gunnery target by the Royal Navy and was sunk on August 16, 1921. However, some reports place her much further out in the Channel.

Bembridge 11 miles; Portsmouth 16 miles.

179 Isleworth. At 50 35 37; 01 13 46. Depth: 51m. Just on the south-west corner of the old explosives dumping ground of St. Catherine's Deep is the

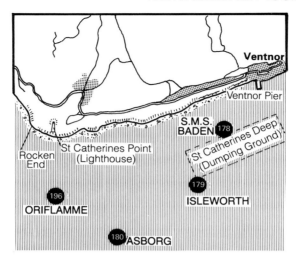

wreck of the *Isleworth,* a 2871-ton steamer laden with iron ore from Bilbao on her way to Middlesbrough, when she was torpedoed on April 30, 1918, by *UC-17* commanded by Oberleutnant Erich Stephan, who had taken over this U-boat when her former commander Ralph Wenniger was promoted to a newer boat. The *Isleworth,* 320ft long with a beam of 46ft, was hit three miles off Ventnor. Though the Captain survived, 29 of her crew died in the sinking.

The British steamer was no stranger to submarines. Built in 1896, she had been in operation for the Britain Steamship Company throughout the war. The previous September she had been chased by a U-boat on the surface to the North of Scotland and had only escaped because of the foul weather and onset of darkness. On January 20, 1918, a torpedo narrowly missed her in the Bristol Channel. This time the torpedo struck her on the starboard side and she sank within seconds.

Today she is upright, but her depth has restricted diving and there is little information about her condition.

Bembridge 12 miles; Portsmouth 17 miles.

180 Asborg. At 50 31 30; 01 15 54. Depth: 20m. Oberleutnant Johann Lohs in *UC-75* noted this one in his log as "a steamer travelling alone with steelplate and coal". Presumably he got this information from questioning the crew in their lifeboats because they were all saved after he put a torpedo into her in the early morning of January 3, 1918. The *Asborg,* a 2750-ton boat built in 1896 by Short Brothers, was Norwegian run at the time of her sinking and was travelling from the Tyne to Leghorn, Italy. She was 320ft long with a beam of 43ft.

Today she is upright, broken, but eight metres proud and lying east to west on a sand and gravel seabed.

Bembridge 14 miles; Portsmouth 19 miles.

181 Camberwell. At 50 31 57; 01 02 48. Depth: 31m. This wreck is thought to be that of the big British steamer *Camberwell*, which sank after hitting a

The Wapello *was torpedoed in 1917 on the way from Philadelphia to Thameshaven. She was loaded with benzine. Courtesy E.N. Taylor.*

mine on May 18, 1917 when she was carrying a general cargo, about ten miles east of St. Catherine's Point. The 4078-ton *Camberwell* measured 368ft with a beam of 50ft. Salvage divers found this wreck in 1973. They reported her as large, lying on her starboard side, and ten metres proud of the seabed of gravel. The ship, they thought, was about 390ft long and lay with her stern to the north-east. There was damage to both bow and stern and her superstructure was missing. She had six large holds, but there appeared to be no cargo in them. Her single large steel propeller was in place. The salvage divers also said that they thought her a little large for the *Camberwell*. There is just a chance that this is in fact the wreck of the *Wapello* (See Site No. 182).

Whatever her name, this is an enjoyable and interesting dive on a big · ship. Nothing had changed since the 1973 reports. The wreck is well defined with the bows fairly intact and both anchors still stowed. The hull is split open amidships from what looks like an explosion. This is a big wreck and takes several dives to see all round it.

Bembridge 11 miles; Portsmouth 16 miles.

182 Wapello. At 50 31 53; 01 01 07. Depth: 25m. This position for a large wreck is only one mile from the site of the *Camberwell* and some people believe that the *Camberwell* site is really the *Wapello*. (See Site No. 181). The *Wapello* was of 5576 tons and is described as an "oiler". She was laden with benzine when she was torpedoed by Oberleutnant Reinhold Salzwedel in *UC-71* on June 15, 1917. The 396ft tanker was coming from Philadelphia and heading for Thameshaven when she was hit. Two men died in the explosion of the torpedo.

This was not the first encounter of the *Wapello* with a submarine. She had been attacked before on her previous voyage over the same route – on April 21 when off the coast of south-west Ireland, but on that occasion the submarine had surfaced and used her gun. The *Wapello* had replied with hers and the submarine had given up the hunt. It was not so simple this time. Salzwedel, whose orders had specifically included "around the Isle of

Wight" as part of his killing ground made no mistake and she sank swiftly.
Bembridge 12 miles; Portsmouth 17 miles.

183 Highland Brigade. At 50 34 50; 01 05 10. Depth: 30m. The *Highland Brigade* was a large merchant steamship of 5669-tons, 385ft long with a beam of 50ft and was built in Glasgow in 1901. She was torpedoed by Oberleutnant Marzecha in *UC-71* on April 7, 1918, south-east of St. Catherine's Point. The stricken ship managed to limp on to a point 3½ miles to the east of Dunnose Point where she finally sank. All the crew were saved.

A large part of the *Highland Brigade's* cargo was tin ingots. In the early 1950's this was a valuable commodity and a certain amount was salvaged during 1953. Later in 1964 salvage operations were started by Risdon Beazley who worked this site on and off till 1970. This wreck now belongs to Island diver Martin Woodward who is still working the site.

The hull of the wreck is still fairly intact and is heeled over to port. The bows have been well flattened to enable the salvage men to reach her cargo. The central superstructure and bridge appear to be missing or have collapsed into the hull. The wreck lies east and west, with its bows to the east. The highest part is the stern which stands some 10m off the seabed. Part of the cargo was telephone equipment as much has been found on the site including candlestick telephones. The binnacle has been recovered. It was caught in a diving boat's grapnel when it was pulled up!
Bembridge 8 miles; Portsmouth 13 miles.

184 UB-81. At 50 29 22; 00 58 12. Depth: 28m. The first mission of this 650-ton U-boat was her last. *UB-81* was brand-new when she left Zeebrugge in the dark of November 28, 1917. In command of this 182ft boat was an old hand at submarine warfare – Reinhold Salzwedel, who ranked 11th in the table of record sinkings of all U-boat captains, having sunk 150,000 tons of Allied shipping in just 12 missions with the Flanders Flotilla. Salzwedel had been decorated many times and was the holder of the coveted "Blue Max", the Pour le Merité cross, Germany's highest war

Laden with tin ingots, Highland Brigade *was torpedoed off St. Catherine's and finally sank east of Dunnose Point. In 1950 some of the valuable cargo was salvaged and the site is still being worked. Courtesy Tom Rayner.*

decoration of the time.

The mission on which *UB-81* set out on that November night was to be Salzwedel's 13th. Even so it did not seem to be unlucky at the start, and carrying ten torpedoes for her four bow and one stern tubes UB-81 slid through the Dover defences without being detected even though she made the run close in at the Folkestone end of the Barrage and over the mine-strewn nets.

Salzwedel wasted no time in getting into action and before midnight on November 30 was attacking a convoy some 12 miles off Beachy Head. He had no success, however, and moved further down Channel. Here he sank a ship he called the "Molesan". She was in fact the armed merchantman *Molesey* of 3218 tons. The *Molesey* stayed afloat long enough for the crew to take to the boats and she is now a Sussex dive at 50 35 23; 00 27 24 where she is upright in 45m.

UB-81 moved on to the west and into a violent storm. The ride on the surface for all 34 men in the U-boat became so uncomfortable that Salzwedel took her down to 20m for a smoother run. At 17.45 on December 2, when the submarine was just two sea miles south of the Owers Lightvessel, a tremendous explosion suddenly threw her sideways. The lights went out and water spurted into the stern compartment.

She sank swiftly downwards and settled heavily on the seabed at 30m. With the added depth the inflow of water increased rapidly, and the only thing to do was to slam the watertight hatch and seal off the rear compartment entirely. But despite the battering the explosion had given the boat, not one of the crew was injured. A swift check of the rest of the submarine showed that apart from the stern, she was undamaged.

What Salzwedel hit must have been a British mine, for the Navy was now well aware of the fondness of German U-boat commanders for the area around lightships, and laid fields accordingly. However, it might have been a German mine laid by another U-boat of the UC class from the Zeebrugge base. It made no difference whose mine had done the damage, for no matter how hard Salzwedel and his engineers tried there seemed no way that *UB-81* would surface.

The water in the flooded stern compartment was pinning her down to the seabed. Finally Salzwedel knew that he could not waste any more precious compressed air in trying to get some buoyancy into his stern tanks. It was clear that the explosion had ruptured them. The boat was lost, so now Salzwedel tried to save his crew.

By pumping all his remaining air into the bow tanks, he hoped that he could raise the bow high enough to get the seaward end of the bow torpedo tubes out of the water and then at least the slimmer members of the crew could get out. All torpedoes were manhandled down to the stern. Torpedoes from loaded bow tubes were withdrawn awkwardly for the boat's bows were already lifting as the air hissed into the forward tanks. Then most of the crew was ordered as far aft as possible. Finally the bow would rise no more. Cautiously, the inside end of the highest bow tube opened. Cold night air rushed into the sub. They had done it! The first man out of the polished tube was Engineer Denker, and he saw how close they had been and still were to disaster. The mouth of the tube was a bare 18 inches above the sea surface, and every moment a wave threatened to break right into it. Quickly, Denker reached down and hoisted Leutnant Freudendahl up on to the slippery slope of the sub's bow. Freudendahl was Salzwedel's second-in-command and as such was to be in charge of the party on the exterior of the submarine. One by one crew members were hauled up – from two tubes now – until there were seven men on the outside and Freudendahl called a halt fearing that any more weight would push the mouth of the tubes under the sea. The sea was getting up again and each swell seemed to hover over the tube openings on each side though the rest of the bow stopped the sea from plunging straight in. It was icy cold out on the casing, and there was no sign of a ship. All was dark, except for the warning flashes from the lightship.

On Salzwedel's orders flare pistols loaded with star shells were discharged into the air and SOS signals flashed by means of a lamp handed up through one of the tubes. But nothing happened, and the men crouched in the cold for hours while their crewmates remained motionless in the stern, straining their ears to catch any of the muffled exchanges between Salzwedel and Freudendahl. Suddenly there was a shout from outside. No one needed telling that an English ship had found them; the noise of engines drummed through the hull. English voices shouted across the water. More engine noises came close as more boats arrived. Outside Freudendahl saw his men transferred to the first English Naval patrol boat to find them. He was last across but before he left he could hear the *UB-81* crew queueing to come up.

He was just speculating about the difficulty which some of the fatter, larger crew members were going to have in the narrow torpedo tubes and wondering whether it would be possible to get them out through the conning tower hatch, which was now not all that far under, when, to his horror, the question became superfluous. One of the British patrol boats, trying to get in close to the stricken sub, was suddenly hurled forward by an exceptionally large wave. The patrol boat's bow bit deep into the U-boat's hull. The screaming hiss of compressed air escaping told it all. Within seconds *UB-81* was gone in a swirl of black water. A moment later great gouts of air burst through the surface in two places from the open torpedo tubes and then there were only the waves hurrying along in the searchlights' beams. There were no more survivors, and it seems likely that Reinhold Salzwedel, the other young lieutenant aboard, and 25 crewmen died very quickly as they would hardly have had the time or the strength to shut the bow tube doors against the December sea.

After the sinking there were British reports which said that only two crewmen escaped through the torpedo tubes, and that a British patrol boat seeing a form emerge, a vague form in the darkness, turned a full speed to ram. The two Germans clinging to the bow waved and shouted, but the patrol boat did not stop. It crashed into the hull and sank the U-boat. The reason for this story is not clear. Perhaps it was part of the propaganda war which was waged at the time – a story to play on the nerves of the rest of the Flanders Flotilla. Certainly the names of all the survivors are given by German sources and they claim it was an accident that caused the British boat to ram the stricken sub. It is hardly likely that they would say this if the sinking had been deliberate.

How long the *UB-81* lay on the seabed in that position no one can know. If there was enough air left in the undamaged bow tank it may be that the tides pushed her around almost at once. Certainly when the Navy looked for her in 1961, she was gone. Then in 1970 she was found at 50 27 00; 00 51 00 – 12 miles from the place where she sank.

In 1974 she was discovered upright on a flat sand and shingle seabed some 14 miles south-east of the Isle of Wight. The diver who found her while working for a salvage firm noted that the only real damage, even though slight, appeared to be to her bow. But when dived in 1989 she was found broken in two just aft of the conning tower, which is itself split in two. Highest point is the gun, barrel pointing to the surface, with ready-use ammunition for the gun all around. Main hatch is open to the control room. Parts of the gun and bridge telegraph have been recovered.
Bembridge 14 miles; Portsmouth 19 miles.

185 Unknown. At 50 26 42; 00 57 39. Depth: 33m. This unknown wreck 15 miles south-east of St. Catherine's Point was first located in 1958 during a survey by *HMS Dalrymple*. Some say she might be the large British steamship *Camberwell* (See Site 181), but there is no evidence to support that theory.
This wreck sits upright and lies east to west. She is nearly 400ft long and is fairly intact except for considerable damage to her bows and mid section. Her large steel propeller is still in place. The holds still have evidence of her cargo which seems to have been mainly bricks, glass and steel tubes. The wreck stands well off the seabed, up to 9m clear.
Bembridge 16 miles; Portsmouth 21 miles.

186 Gerarda. Positively identified in 1989 by her bell, this 1673-ton iron steamer, 257ft long with a beam of 34ft, sailed on her maiden voyage from Shields for Genoa with a cargo of coal on October 21, 1882. In the early hours of October 24 in stormy weather she collided with the homeward-bound Glasgow barque *Benares* for London from Calcutta. The *Benares'* bows were badly damaged, but the *Gerarda* was worse hit and started sinking. Fourteen of her crew were rescued, but eight men and her Master, Captain D. Johnston, died.
Today she lies at 50 30 50; 00 55 54 in 30m. She is broken in two. Most recognisable is the stern, which is upside down and 6-7m proud. Her four-bladed steel propeller of 12ft diameter is still in place. The port side is fairly intact, but the starboard is breaking up showing her boiler and engine room. Both anchors lie off the wreck, together with her winches and chains.
Bembridge 13 miles; Portsmouth 17 miles.

187 Fallodon. At 50 26 00; 01 06 00. Depth: 30m. "Five torpedoes, five kills", exulted Oberleutnant Steindorff in *UC-71* in his log after seeing the 3011-ton *Fallodon* sink on December 28, 1917. Certainly Steindorff had made his Christmas mission from 22-30 December a sad one for the Allies with 15,658 tons of shipping sunk.
The *Fallodon* was on her way from Le Havre, bound for Glasgow in ballast. She sank about 12 miles off St. Catherine's Point with the loss of one of the crew. Built by Bartram and Sons in 1903 for the London and Northern Steamship Company, the *Fallodon* was 339ft long with a beam of 48ft. There are no reports available of the diving on her.
Bembridge 17 miles; Portsmouth 23 miles.

188 Unknown. At 50 27 00; 01 11 42. Depth: 36m. An unknown ship was reported as having sunk in this approximate position 8½ miles south-east of St. Catherine's Point. No sign of any wreck has been found.
Bembridge 17 miles; Portsmouth 23 miles.

HMS Swordfish *hit a mine south of St. Catherine's Point in 1940. Her fate was not known until 1983 when Martin Woodward found her. Her position is secret and she is an official war grave.*

189 Unknown. At 50 25 00; 01 10 00. Depth: 35m. An unknown ship was reported sunk in this position by the steamship *Blydendyks* who saw a mast awash here, 11 miles south-east of St. Catherine's Point in 1924. The area was surveyed in 1957, but no sign of a wreck was found.

Bembridge 19 miles; Portsmouth 24 miles.

190 HMS Swordfish, off St. Catherine's Point. Depth: 50m. Actual position is secret. *HMS Swordfish* was the first of the 'S' submarines. She was laid down at Chatham Dockyard on December 1, 1930 and was launched on November 10, 1931 by Lady Tyrwhitt. The submarine had an overall length of 202ft and a beam of 24ft. When surfaced she had a draught of 11ft forward and 13ft aft. Her standard displacement was 640-tons. Her engines produced 1,550b.h.p., and the electric motors 1,300h.p. Her performance was good, on the surface with a top speed of 14 knots and a cruising speed of 9 knots at which she had a range of 3,800 miles. Submerged, her top speed was 10 knots but at this speed her endurance was only one hour. At two knots she could stay down for 36 hours, and her maximum operating depth was 300ft. She was well armed with six 21″ torpedo tubes, all in the bow and in addition there was a 3″ gun and a .303 Lewis gun.

HMS Swordfish left Portsmouth for her 12th patrol, under the command of Lt Michael Langley on November 7, 1940. Her destination was the French coast near Ushant, where she was to relieve the submarine *Usk*. The *Swordfish* disappeared. For many years it was believed that she had been lost somewhere near Ushant, probably falling prey to a German destroyer.

In 1983 Island diver Martin Woodward found the remains of the submarine a few miles south of St. Catherine's Point. It appeared to have hit a mine, probably shortly after diving. The hull is broken into two sections. The bow from the gun forward lies on its port side and the stern sits upright. Her bridge telegraphs were found still set at 'slow ahead'. The aft escape hatch was found open, so it is possible some of her crew were able to make an escape from the doomed boat, but none survived. The position of the wreck of the Swordfish – a war grave – is a closely-guarded secret known only to Martin Woodward and the Royal Navy.

Area Information and services

Admiralty Charts: 2045 (Outer Approaches to the Solent). 2219 (Western Approaches to the Solent).

Ordnance Survey: 196.

Local weather: (0898) 500403. Marinecall (0898) 500457. For mid-channel forecast. Southampton Weather Centre. Southampton (0703) 28844.

Local coastguard: 999 (emergencies). At sea VHF Channel 16. Solent Coastguard, Lee-on-Solent (0705) 552100.

Local BS-AC Branches: Yaverland No. 1472. This is a small branch who hold their dry meetings on Sunday lunchtimes at the Yaverland Sailing Club, Yaverland, Sandown. They welcome visiting divers to join them on dives when possible. Contact: Tracy Tompkinson (0983) 812033.

Accommodation: See Area One.

Air supplies: Dolphin Enterprises, The Workshop, Mitchell Avenue, Ventnor, I.O.W. Tel: (0983) 527782. Run by Dave Woodford. Supplies air to 3500 psi, sales and service, hours by arrangement.

Other services: See previous areas.

Area 6: St. Catherine's Point to Freshwater Bay

This section runs from 01 17 00 to the west to link up with Area One at 01 33 00. To the south the area reaches to the edge of Chart No. 2045. This means that the whole of the Back of the Wight with many of the ships lost under those steep cliffs is included in this section and we have come full circle round the Island.

Where there were not huge towering cliffs for the old-time sailor to become embayed, there were dangerous reefs stretching out up to one and a half miles offshore. These ship-rippers run along the front of the cliffs all the way from St. Catherine's Point to Hanover Point. The only real break in the cliffs comes at Freshwater Gate, mid-way between Hanover Point and the Needles.

A 17th century astrolabe was found by Martin Woodward in 15m off St. Catherine's Point in 1986. This part of the coast is one long story of shipwreck after shipwreck. Divers with treasure on their minds should remember the name Chale Bay – between Atherfield Point and Blackgang Chine. For it is in those two miles that "Armada" coins have been washed ashore. "Armada" in this context means pieces of eight. No one has yet located the shipwreck from which they have come, but then, the whole of this section of the Back of the Wight is difficult to explore. All diving must be boat diving and there is no shelter from strong southerly or south-westerly winds. Many wreck sites are close in – which means coming in among the same reefs which have destroyed so many ships.

The tides too, have helped with the wrecking of those ships. For example, the flood tide in the area has a tendency to set in towards the Brook and Atherfield Ledges, especially during times of strong westerly winds. So the short stretch of coastline from Atherfield Point across Chale Bay and on to the most southerly point of the Island at St. Catherine's – some three miles in all – is one of the largest ships' graveyards in the world. Some say that over 1,000 ships lie around the coasts of the Wight. If that is true many of those ships are here at the Back. And it is true that divers in this area will come across scattered wreckage almost everywhere.

One of the first recorded wrecks here was the *St. Mary of Bayonne*. This small French ship was carrying a cargo of 147 barrels of white wine which was intended for delivery in Picardy. But so strong were the winds that she was blown all the way north and finally ran ashore in Chale Bay on April 22, 1313. As might be expected the news of the wreck spread fast, and the locals were soon on the spot buying or stealing the wine from the crew. Even the Lord of Chale, Walter De Godeton, was there, removing wine. We

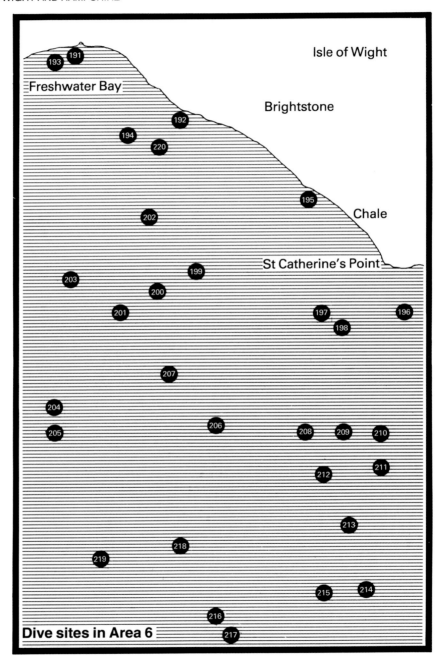

Isle of Wight

Freshwater Bay

Brightstone

Chale

St Catherine's Point

Dive sites in Area 6

know that because there is a record of the court in which he was arraigned and heavily fined.

It was the wreck of another ship many years later – at Blackgang Chine – which led to the erection of St. Catherine's Lighthouse. On October 11, 1836, the *Clarendon*, a three-master of 345 tons, returning from the West Indies with a crew of 16 and ten passengers, was driven on shore by mountainous seas. Some idea of the violent conditions can be imagined when you know that the whole ship was smashed to pieces by just four waves! Local fishermen, led by one John Wheeler, worked heroically to rescue three of the crew – but all the rest were lost.

The sight of the broken and mangled bodies recovered from the surf, laid out along the beach – there were two little girls among the victims – caused such a local uproar and public outcry that work on the lighthouse began the very next year. It was completed in 1840.

St. Catherine's Lighthouse. A small light was first set up at St. Catherine's in about 1323 by Walter de Godeton (the same Sir Walter who was earlier fined for looting a wreck!) Sir Walter erected a chapel, appointed a priest to say Masses for the Godeton family and added to the priest's duties the showing of lights to warn ships away from this dangerous coast. This continued until about 1530, when the endowment was swallowed up in the Reformation.

The present light was completed and the light first shown in March, 1840. The lighthouse is near to the site of Sir Walter's chapel at Niton Undercliffe, five miles from Ventnor. The first tower was too high and often became mist-covered, so in 1875 the light was lowered 43 feet by taking out a section of 20 feet from the upper section and another 23 feet out of the middle tier. The tower is now 26 metres high and the main light, giving one flash every five seconds, is 42 metres above High Water. It has a candle power of 5,250,000 and is visible up to 30 miles. A fixed red subsidiary light is displayed from a window 7 metres below the main light and shows westward over the Atherfield Ledges. This can be seen for 16 miles.

The fog signal house used to be near the cliff edge, but erosion caused such serious cracks that in 1932 the signal was moved to a lower tower, annexed to the front of the lighthouse and gives a three-second blast every 45 seconds. The small tower was built as a replica of the main structure. Locals call them "The Cow and the Calf".

Tides are strong. In the western part of the area the flood tide reaches around two knots on Springs and this gradually increases as the tide approaches St. Catherine's Point, where the speed can reach four-and-a-half knots. Similarly in the western area, inshore of the 20m line, the flood tide may be about one knot, but it increases as it approaches St. Catherine's. The ebb works the opposite way. Off St. Catherine's it can reach four knots, but it gradually reduces as it travels west, and once again the tides are less strong inshore of the 20m line. Slack water occurs at one hour before and five hours after High Water Portsmouth.

Launch sites

Brook Point. Only for small inflatables. See Brook Ledges (Site No. 192).

Freshwater Bay. Not to be confused with the town of Freshwater, which is well inland. At the Bay there is a small wooden slipway which has been built to allow the launching of the Freshwater Inshore Rescue boat across the

St. Catherine's Lighthouse has a history dating back to 1323. The fog signal house is a replica of the lighthouse. The pair are known locally as 'The Cow and the Calf'.

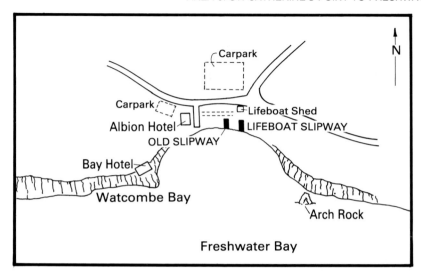

shingle beach. Permission can sometimes be obtained to use it to launch small boats. There is a large car park across the road from the beach and there is a small cafe close by and the Albion Hotel.

Shore diving sites

191 Freshwater Bay. There is easy access for the diver to the water here, but the diving is not particularly interesting. The floor of the bay is mainly sand and shingle, with a maximum depth of 10m. There are areas of rock around the seaward edges of the bay which carry a large amount of seaweed. Divers should keep clear of the area of the lifeboat launch slip and, though there is practically no tidal movement in the bay itself, there can be an uncomfortable swell rolling onto the beach. Several small boats moor in the Bay during the summer months. SMB's should be used.

192 Brook Ledges. These cover some two miles of the Islands south-west coastline. This area is a veritable graveyard of old ships and from the earliest recorded days of shipping, wrecks have happened here. The whole area seems to be littered with bits and pieces of ships. Divers have picked up all manner of ships' fittings from this area including a ship's sextant and sounding leads. Diver Dougie Saunders was snorkelling over the western end of the Ledges one evening in shallow water, when he saw below him, jammed between some rocks, a timber hull. The shape was quite clear and there were timbers sticking out of the sand. All around were large copper pins that once held the planks together. She would be worth looking for again when the sand has shifted.

There is a car park at Brook Point and a pathway down to the beach. The path is gated just above the beach but it is possible to lift small inflatable boats over this and launch off the beach. This is a very interesting diving area. The water is shallow with a maximum depth of 10m. The visibility is usually good except when an onshore wind stirs up the sand close in.

First set on fire in a collision with an American tanker, the War Knight *finally succumbed after hitting a German mine in 1918. Courtesy Blackgang Chine Museum.*

Boat diving sites

193 War Knight. At 50 39 54; 01 31 02. Depth 15m. The wreck of this 410ft large armed steamer of 7951 tons lies less than a quarter-mile from the centre of Freshwater Bay. She came to a terrible end. On March 24, 1918, the British ship was homeward-bound from Philadelphia, U.S.A. She was part of a large convoy coming up-Channel at night with no lights burning. Keeping station in the darkness was difficult, but the convoy had been warned that there were German submarines about. For some reason the *O.B. Jennings* an American tanker in the convoy, turned across the *War Knight's* bows. The *Jennings* of 10,300 tons was fully laden with a cargo of the highly-inflammable naptha oil. The collision set off the naptha and both ships were enveloped in flames. Thirty-two men died in the fire, almost the whole of the crews of both ships.

The ships were soon taken in tow by escorting destroyers, even though the *Jennings* was blazing fiercely. The *War Knight's* troubles were not over. As she was towed in, she struck a mine laid by a German U-boat to catch Portsmouth and Southampton shipping and her own supplies of ammunition started exploding. The destroyer pulled her as quickly as possible into the nearest shallow water – off Freshwater Bay – and sank her with gunfire in the hope that she could be salvaged later.

The *O.B. Jennings* was towed right round to Sandown Bay and anchored there. She burned fiercely for four days before the Navy put a torpedo into her to sink her and put the fire out. She was later raised, repaired and joined an outward-bound convoy for America, but she was again torpedoed, this time by a German U-boat when just 100 miles from New York. This time she sank in deep water for good.

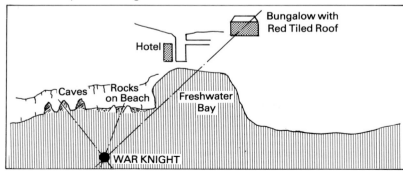

Marks for the War Knight. (Site 193).

The Navy had been right when it had warned the convoy that there were submarines about. In fact there was one very close indeed.

Kapitanleutnant Fritz Wassner, a German U-boat ace who had already sunk nearly 100,000 tons of Allied shipping, was more than surprised by the explosion. He had fired no torpedoes. In his log he wrote: "24.3. Close to *UB-59*, a loud detonation with high flames. Oil from a tanker is burning." To this entry he later added: "We later found out that it was the result of a collision between the English steamer *War Knight*, 7951 t. with the American steamer *O.B. Jennings*, 10300 t. The English steamer later ran on to one of the mines laid by *UC-17* by the Needles."

When the *War Knight* finally sank, her hull split open and much of her cargo spilled out. Sides of bacon and 28lb slabs of lard soon washed up on the beaches, much to the delight of the locals. She was too badly damaged to refloat. Some years later she was heavily salvaged which has left the wreck very flattened. The only parts standing up are small sections of the hull, the boiler and the bows, which are three metres proud of the seabed. Piles of anchor chain are hanging out of the chain locker. Although well broken, she makes an interesting dive over a wide area. The seabed is mainly sand and shingle with some outcrops of rock, particularly one large rock some 100 yards to the north of the site. This rock never shows above water. The wreck lies north-north-west to south-south-east and has a half-metre scour on one side. Small boats can be launched from Freshwater Bay and be on the site in minutes. Some divers swim out from the beach at Watcombe Bay, but this can be dangerous, for if the ebb tide catches them there is nothing but sheer cliffs for three miles to the West.

Yarmouth 8 miles; Lymington 9.5 miles.

194 Juno. At 50 38 00; 01 28 00. Depth: Not known. This position is a very, very approximate guess. All that is really known of the position of this Dutch frigate of 36 guns is that she was wrecked off Sudmoor Point on December 9 or 10, 1786 when homeward bound from the East Indies.

Reports of the loss of life vary from six to over 100, but the lesser figure is probably correct. She has not been located by divers to the authors' knowledge, though there are tales current on the Island saying that some of her cargo has been found.

Most gripping account of her loss is given by *The Times* of December 15, 1786, who printed on that day a "Letter from Cowes, December 13". This reads: "On the night of the 10th inst. the Juno, Dutch frigate of 36 guns and 250 men, Captain De Wits, from the East Indies to Holland, was drove on shore at Sodmore on the south-west part of the Isle of Wight; four of the men came on shore upon a raft, and in attempting to go off to the ship in a fishing boat, the boat overset and three of the men were drowned, and after that eleven men came ashore, on another raft, who were near two hours coming on shore; the ship distant about a mile from the shore.

"A reward was offered by R. Bull, Esq, to any person that would get on board her, when a smuggling boat put off, but could not get near the ship; and had it not been for the said smuggling boat the above eleven men would not have got to shore as soon as they did. The raft on which they were being checked by the eddy tide. Whether any more of the people are got on shore is not yet known here. Wind south-west blows hard."

There is more information in the log of James Wheeler, an ex-Navy sailor and local fisherman of Chale Bay. He records some 60 wrecks from 1746 to 1808.

Auguste. This three-masted iron German barque hit the eastern side of Atherfield Ledges in 1900 and became a total loss. All the crew was saved. Courtesy Blackgang Chine Museum.

Of the *Juno*, he wrote that she struck at five in the morning of December 9 and that she ran ashore "at Sudmore Point in a storm at south by east". He adds that she had on board a "great quantity of handkerchiefs, pieces of silk, clothes and money, and other things of great value were lost, and five or six men were drowned". He later added another note: "The wreck was sold for £444". That was a vast sum for those days and one wonders what a Dutch East Indiaman warship of 900 tons would have on board which made her wreckage worth so much!

Yarmouth 10 miles; Lymington 11 miles.

195 Auguste. At 50 37 00; 01 22 00. Depth: 8m. This three-masted iron-hulled German barque of 1298 tons left Freemantle, Western Australia with a cargo of Jarrah wood intended to be made into wood blocks to pave London's roads. But the wood ended up spread along the beaches of the southern coast of the Isle of Wight when Captain Ammerman's ship drove on to the eastern side of Atherfield Ledges in a southerly gale and low visibility on February 15, 1900.

The Atherfield lifeboat was launched, but at first was unable to make any headway against the giant seas lashing the beach. It was not until ten hours later that the gale shifted direction slightly and the lifeboat finally got away. All 18 crew and Captain Ammerman were saved by the lifeboat, but the ship was a total loss.

Today she lies alongside the Ledge and is well split up, but it is possible to swim inside one section where the waterlogged remains of some of her cargo can still be seen.

Yarmouth 4 miles; Lymington 15 miles.

196 Oriflamme. At 50 33 12; 01 17 48. Depth: 33m. Built of steel in 1899 she was one of the early steam tankers. During her war service she had a gun on the stern of her 336ft hull. She was bound for Le Havre from New York and laden with benzine when, on November 25, 1917, she hit a mine nine miles south of the Nab Lightvessel and burst into flames. Even so tugs managed to tow the 3764 ton tanker some distance until she finally sank just a mile south of St. Catherine's Point.

The *Oriflamme* now lies on her port side with her bow pointing to the north-east. Her highest point is the stern 8m above the fine sand seabed. She is very broken and has been swept.

There is a rocky ledge about 300 yards east of the site with a depth of 25m over it, which can be mistaken for the wreck on an echo-sounder.

Bembridge 14 miles; Portsmouth 19 miles.

197 Tank Landing Craft. At 50 33 12; 01 21 44. Depth: 41m. This wreck was first found in 1972. She lies east to west and is upright 3m proud of the sand and gravel seabed.

Yarmouth 16 miles; Lymington 17 miles.

198 Unknown. At 50 33 10; 01 21 06. Depth: 55m. At first thought to be the *Molina* – until that ship was positively identified by her bell (see 201). This wreck of a small steamer stands upright, deep and some six metres proud on hard sand with just a slight scour around her.

Yarmouth 16.5 miles; Lymington 17.5 miles.

199 Westville. At 50 34 18; 01 26 36. Depth: 29m. Not a Happy New Year for this British steamer of 3207 tons, for she was torpedoed on New Year's Eve, 1917 when carrying 4965 tons of coal from Blyth to Blaye, on the Gironde near Bordeaux, France. She was 7 miles west-north-west of St. Catherine's Light when the torpedo, fired from *UB-35* by Oberleutnant K. Stöter, hit her. Stöter had fired from the surface using the steel snout of his boat as a foresight for his aim. The hit was mortal, but the 335ft steamer stayed afloat along enough for the crew to take to the boats without casualties. She now lies with her bows to the north-west, six metres proud of the seabed broken, but upright.

Yarmouth 12 miles; Lymington 14 miles.

Torpedoed on New Year's Eve, 1917, the Westville *was carrying coal from Blyth to Blaye, near Bordeaux. Courtesy E.N. Taylor.*

200 Unknown. At 50 34 11; 01 27 43. Depth: 30m. This wreck is a bit of a mystery. Located in 1980, she appeared to be a modern wreck about 240ft long and standing 8m high with a mast still standing. She lies north-west and south-east six-and-a-half miles west of St. Catherine's Point. It is just possible that this is the wreck of the 1028 ton British coaster *'Pool Fisher'* which capsized and sank in heavy weather on November 6, 1979, although she is listed as being elsewhere (see 206). It would be worth a dive to clear this one up.

Yarmouth 13 miles; Lymington 15 miles.

201 Molina. At 50 33 46; 01 28 58. Depth: 35m. Built in 1905, this 1122 ton Norwegian steamer was torpedoed by Oberleutnant Stöter in *UB-35* on the same day as he sank the *Serrana* (Site 12). The *Molina* was going from Le Havre to Swansea in ballast on January 22, 1918 when she was torpedoed some 7 miles south-east of the Needles. The 229ft ship, with her 109 hp engines, is today an excellent dive. She is still fairly intact and definitely ship-shaped, standing well off the bottom and some eight metres proud. She lies with her bows to the north-west and was positively identified by her bell, recovered by a diver in 1985. But take care when diving her – the plates are becoming very thin and could start collapsing at any time. A propellor with two blades missing was recovered by salvage divers.

Yarmouth is 12 miles; Lymington 13 miles.

202 Witte Zee. At 50 35 50; 01 28 24. Depth: 32m. The 328 ton *Witte Zee* was an ocean-going tug belonging to the famous towing and salvage company Smit & Co. and was based at Rotterdam in Holland. She was built in 1943 and measured 122ft by 25ft by 14ft.

On February 23, 1964, the 7300 ton freighter *Brother George* ran ashore on the Brook Ledges whilst on a voyage from Manchester to her home port, also Rotterdam. Several tugs were soon on the scene hoping for the salvage contract, but it was the *Witte Zee* which was awarded it.

Master of the tug was Captain Klein. He soon closed in on the freighter with his crew waiting to fire a towing line. Just as they were about to fire the tow line a particularly large wave rolled up behind the tug and crashed over her stern. She rolled heavily and was sluggish to right herself. The reason for this was that her bow had been holed on the rocks of Brook Ledge and water was rushing in. Captain Klein quickly decided that he should head for the safety of the Solent for repairs. It soon became apparent however that the hull was flooding fast and help was called. Luckily the other tugs and the Yarmouth Lifeboat *"Earl and Countess Howe"* were close by. The tug *Gatcombe* took off eight of the crew and the tug *Abielle* took the sinking boat in tow. By the time the lifeboat was alongside, the decks of the *Witte Zee* were awash and the remainder of the crew soon abandoned ship. Two hours later the stricken tug disappeared beneath the waves, four-and-a-half miles south of Freshwater Bay.

Plans to salvage the tug in 1965 never materialised. She now lies north to south, bows to the north. The wreck stands 6-7m off the seabed. There is a shallow scour around the site. The hull is breaking open in places.

Yarmouth 13 miles; Lymington 15 miles.

203 Unknown. At 50 33 51; 01 31 49. Depth: 40m. This "unknown" was first located in 1945 6 miles south of Freshwater Bay. It was first dived in April 1965 and the divers' report stated that the wreck was well broken up and

HMS Upstart *was sunk as a target in 1957. She was located by divers in 1975.*

appeared to consist of mainly loose girders and ribs. She was approximately 30ft long and stood 5m high. More recent dives show that the wreck was at least 150 feet long and stood some 6.5m high off the seabed of stone and sand. There is a deep scour of some 2.5m along the side of the wreck. The site lies in a north-east – south-west direction.

It is possible that the wreckage first found was just a portion of the main wreckage or, of course, may be that of another shipwreck entirely.

Yarmouth 11 miles; Lymington 12 miles.

204 Unknown. At 50 30 30; 01 32 28. Depth: 35m. This site was first thought to be that of *HMS Acheron*, but recent diving has revealed it to be the wreck of a small coaster or large trawler. She is lying on her port side, north to south, and five metres proud. Not an easy dive, as she lies across the tide. This site is not far from the wreck of *HMS Upstart* (see 205).

Yarmouth 13 miles; Lymington 14 miles.

205 HM Submarine Upstart. At 50 30 22; 01 32 45. Depth: 35m. This site, 9.5 miles south of the Needles, is definitely a submarine, and is probably *HMS Upstart* (ex-P65), a U-class submarine of 740 tons and 197ft long. She was sunk as an asdic target on July 29 1957. She was located by divers in 1975, who thought she might be the British submarine *A3*, but she sank on the Princessa Shoal in 1912 and was subsequently salvaged.

The wreck is partly buried in the shingle seabed, and is heeled over to port. She lies east and west with her bows to the east. The conning-tower is of round construction, and is the highest point standing 8m off the bottom. The tower hatch is open, as is another one on the aft deck. The pressure hull appears to be in good condition. Her gun and both propellers are missing.

Yarmouth 14.5 miles; Lymington 16 miles.

The Pool Fisher *was carrying potash in November 1979, when she sank, probably because the No. 1 hatch was not properly secured. Courtesy Tom Rayner.*

206 Pool Fisher. At 50 30 18; 01 25 57. Depth: 37m. A British MV of 1028 tons, the *Pool Fisher* was carrying a cargo of potash on November 6, 1979 when the 218ft ship overturned in gale force winds. The ship was on her way from Hamburg to Runcorn. It is believed she sank because No. 1 hatch cover was not properly secured.

The bottom on which the ship now lies is extremely uneven to say the least, with depths plunging up and down between 37m and 50m. The *Pool Fisher* is swept clear by chains at 37m but no further diving information is available.

Yarmouth 17 miles; Lymington 18 miles.

207 HMS Acheron. At 50 32 00; 01 26 00. Depth: 48m. As 149 men died in her sinking in December, 1940, this British destroyer is most likely to be designated under the Military Remains Act as a war grave and divers should take careful note of this.

The Admiralty announced her loss on December 26, 1940, nine days after her sinking. She struck a German mine in the bitter cold of the early morning of December 17. The 1350 ton destroyer had left Portsmouth for high-speed trials south of the Isle of Wight following a refit. She carried a full complement of 190 and 25 dockyard men were also aboard. Her captain was Lieutenant R. J. Wilson.

The *Acheron* was 323ft long with a beam of 32.2ft and a draught of 12ft. She had been built by Thornycroft in 1930 and with her 34,000 hp turbine engines could reach a speed of 35 knots. She carried four 4.7 guns, two 2-pounders, five machine-guns and had eight torpedo tubes.

HMS Acheron was just beginning a turn to the east when "there was a muffled roar and the darkness was transformed to brilliant light as she erupted into flame" said one survivor. The suddenness of the explosion, which blew her in two, is made clear by the story of Stoker Reg Willis who told how he climbed out of the escape hatch and "I saw the bow was missing. I just jumped – there was nothing else to do!" The pieces of the *Acheron* sank swiftly. Lieutenant Wilson and other officers and 145 ratings

Twenty-five luckless dockyard men went down with the complement of 190 officers and men when HMS Acheron *struck a German mine in the bitter December chill of 1940. Courtesy Maritime Photo Library.*

were lost. Another two officers and 13 ratings were wounded.

The position given here is an Admiralty one and is only approximate. The *Acheron* was pinpointed by the well-known Isle of Wight diver, Martin Woodward, in 1984. He found the two sections about a quarter of a mile apart.

Yarmouth 15 miles; Lymington 18 miles.

208 Redesmere. At 50 29 56; 01 21 27. Depth: 37m. The 2123 ton *Redesmere* was on her way from Barry to Southampton with a cargo of 3300 tons of coal on October 28, 1917, when she was torpedoed by Oberleutnant Howaldt in *UB-40*. The attack on this 290ft steamer with a beam of 43ft was so sudden that 19 men died and when her captain reported the loss to the owners, the Watson Steamship Company, he said that they had been

This ship, the Redesmere, *was carrying coal when she was mined or torpedoed west-south-west of St. Catherine's with the loss of 19 crew. Courtesy E.N. Taylor.*

"mined or torpedoed six miles west-south-west of St. Catherine's Point".

The steamer, which was built by the Sunderland Shipbuilding Company in 1911, is upright standing five metres proud of the gravel and sand seabed. She lies north to south. There is a metre deep scour along her east side.

Bembridge 20 miles; Portsmouth 25 miles.

209 Ashanti. At 50 30 00; 01 20 00. Depth: 40m. Built in 1936 by the Goole Shipbuilding and Repairing Company, the 534-ton *Ashanti* fitted with a 102 hp oil engine, was a British ship belonging to T.E. Evans and Company but taken over as a supply ship for the Normandy landings of 1944. She was 184ft with a beam of 27ft. On June 10, 1944, the *Ashanti* made her way to the Isle of Wight convoy assembly point. The day before the first ships to form part of the Mulberry Harbour at Arromanches had been sunk in position and *Ashanti* was to be one of the first ships to use this artificial harbour and unload vital supplies for the Allied armies pushing inland. Her cargo was vital. She was packed with jerricans of petrol for the tanks.

At 3.10 am, as she waited for the rest of the convoy in the assembly point 35 miles north of the Mulberry Harbour in France and well south of St. Catherine's Point, death in the shape of a German E-boat came out of the dark. The torpedo went home and no one needed telling what the *Ashanti* carried. The explosion and flame was seen for miles. No one could survive and her crew of ten and seven gunners were all lost.

No diving information is yet available and the position given is only approximate.

Bembridge 17; Portsmouth 22.5 miles.

210 Londonier. At 50 29 58; 01 19 16. Depth: 37m. This 1870 ton Belgian merchantman of the Lloyd Royal Belge line was torpedoed in the morning darkness from a surface position by Oberleutnant Marzecha in command of *UC-71* on March 13, 1918. This was only Marzecha's second mission captaining a U-boat. The crew of the Belgian ship were all saved.

The 279ft *Londonier* was built in 1911 and today sits upright on a hard sand bottom from which she is five metres proud. She lies north-east to south-west and is very broken.

Bembridge 16 miles; Portsmouth 21 miles.

211 HMT Crestflower. At 50 29 02; 01 18 53. Depth: 35m. A 367 ton H.M. trawler, this 150ft ship was built in 1930 and used by the Navy, who bought her in August, 1939, as a mine-sweeper. She foundered after being badly damaged in an air attack on July 21, 1940. Two ratings on board were killed. She now stands upright 8m proud of the hard sand seabed and is breaking up badly.

Bembridge 17 miles; Portsmouth 22 miles.

212 Braat II. At 50 28 50; 01 21 02. Depth: 38m. A Norwegian ship of 1834 tons with a length of 265ft and a beam of 42ft, the *Braat II* was built in 1914 at the Fredriksstad Mek. Verks. At the time of her sinking the ship was in the English Channel heading from Newport for Rouen with a cargo of 2780 tons of Welsh coal. On March 7, 1918, Kapitanleutnant Rhein in *UB-30* torpedoed her with a surface shot in the early morning. The *Braat's* crew all landed safely at Portsmouth after being picked up from their boats by a Navy patrol boat. *UB-30* did not survive the war, being rammed and depth-charged off Whitby when commanded by Oberleutnant Stier on

Happy Island diver John McIntyre pictured with a brass lamp and a shellcase from HMS Mendi.

August 13, 1918. There were no survivors.

Today divers report that the *Braat II* is upright with her bows to the east and stands 6m proud of the gravel seabed. Her holds are still full of coal.

Bembridge 20 miles; Portsmouth 25 miles.

213 Mendi. At 50 27 28; 01 19 54. Depth: 40m. This is listed as the wreck of a lighter, but recent diving revealed something completely different. This is really the wreck of a big steamer sitting on a seabed of hard sand and all indications are that this is the Royal Mail Steamer *Mendi*, which sank on February 20, 1917 with a huge loss of life.

The *Mendi* was used on the Cape-West Africa-Liverpool run and that February was carrying some 800 black South African labourers to France, where they were to be used on the construction of gun sites and other defence works behind the front lines.

At 5 a.m. with fog adding to the pitch black before dawn, the *Mendi* and her destroyer escort were some seven miles off St Catherine's Point when the steamer *Darro* sliced into the *Mendi's* starboard side. The *Mendi* sank swiftly without being able to launch her boats and 650 of the crew and labourers aboard died in the icy cold sea.

Today the wreck lies in a north-east to south-west direction and is over 12m proud. She is breaking up. Much of the decking has collapsed and this

145

RMS Mendi. *Almost certainly the wreck of this large steamer, previously thought to have been a lighter, (Site 213) has recently been re-assessed.*

leaves her large boiler standing above the main wreckage, in which there are many cases of shells and rifle ammunition. Her distinctive square portholes can be seen but most are still well attached. Some Wight divers call this one "Sainsbury's" – it is so easy to fill your bags as you swim along the length of her!

Bembridge 19; Portsmouth 24 miles.

214 Tweed. At 50 25 54; 01 19 36. Depth: 35m. *UB-59* was on the surface in the deep dark of the early morning of March 13, 1918 when she fired one torpedo at the 1025 ton steamer *Tweed*, which was on her way from Newhaven to Cherbourg with general cargo. The British steamer, 230ft long with a beam of 32ft, was eight miles south-west of St. Catherine's Point at the time and sank swiftly, so quickly in fact that seven men died in her. Kapitanleutnant Fritz Wassner of *UB-59* carefully noted in his log that she was in the service of the Admiralty at the time. This careful notation was probably due to the fact that he had already been listed by the British Government as a war criminal for sinking an unarmed steamer without warning the previous year.

Divers researching the *Tweed* should be warned that a ship of exactly the same name, though slightly larger at 1777 tons, was torpedoed and sunk the very next day by Lohs in *UC-75* in the St. George's Channel.

Today the *Tweed*, which was built in 1892 by D.J. Dunlop and Company, stands 8m proud of the seabed. A brass bell has been recovered by divers, but it was unmarked.

Bembridge 19; Portsmouth 24 miles.

215 Mulberry Harbour Unit. At 50 25 45; 01 20 42. Depth: 38m. This site, nine miles south of St. Catherine's Point, is a large section of Mulberry Harbour, lost during Operation Neptune, when dozens of these floating harbour sections were towed across the English Channel to the Normandy beaches.

This one is a steel section around 120ft long, lying in an east-west direction and standing some 7m off the sandy seabed.

Yarmouth 22 miles; Lymington 23 miles.

216 Iduna and **217 South Western.** At 50 25 00; 01 25 30. Depth: 36m. This is the official position of both wrecks. First to settle down on that particular piece of the seabed was the three-masted sailing steamship *Iduna*, of 860 tons built in 1868, which sank after a collision while carrying a cargo of coal from North Shields. All 170 feet of her landed upright on the hard sand.

Next to arrive was the *South Western*. She was built in 1874 by J. and W. Dudgeon for the London and South Western Railway Company, and she went down to the same seabed on March 16, 1918. She was a victim of Kapitanleutnant Fritz Wassner in *UB-59*. An armed British steamer of 674 tons, the *South Western* nearly escaped. Wassner had spotted her first in the early dusk, alone and on course for St. Malo from Southampton with general cargo. Wassner's first torpedo missed. The *South Western* appeared not to notice and ploughed on into the night. Wassner noted her as on course for Cherbourg in his log and set off after her. When he found her again it was just before midnight and she was still on the same course about nine miles south-west-by-south from St. Catherine's Point.

Wassner fired again. This time there was no mistake. The explosion of the torpedo sent the whole of the forepart of the ship flying up into the air. Despite this she floated for 20 minutes until Wassner finally saw her sink. Twenty-four of the crew of the *South Western* died in the explosion and the sinking. The ship was 222ft, with a beam of 27ft.

Many years later strong sonar traces were plotted by a dive boat in the area, which were believed to come from the *South Western*. But when the site was dived in 1975, the boilers and engines which stood some five metres high were not those of the *South Western* at all.

The wreckage on which the divers found themselves was of a wooden hull about 170ft, lying east to west. Amid the wreckage lay the ship's bell. This bore the name "IDUNA".

There can be no argument about her identity. But where is the *South Western?* She is probably very close by, but only more diving will give us the answer.

Bembridge 20 miles; Portsmouth 25 miles.

218 The Double Ender. At 50 26 58; 01 26 58. Depth: 38m. Called this by salvage divers, this is a double-ended ship of some kind, sitting upright. She has no upperworks and appears to be just a hull, though there is some wreckage close by to the south which may have been some sort of bridge. She is 6m proud of the hard sand seabed and lies east to west. More diving information is needed for proper identification.

Yarmouth 19 miles; Lymington 22 miles.

219 Espagne. At 50 26 23; 01 29 25. Depth: 37m. This Belgian steamship of 1463 tons got no mercy from Oberleutnant Steindorff in *UC-71* – even if it was Christmas Day. Perhaps Steindorff was in a temper because he noted in his log that earlier that Christmas morning in 1917 he had failed to sink the *Hyacinthus* of 5756 tons despite hitting her with a torpedo and she had reached harbour "south of the Isle of Wight".

The *Espagne*, 236ft with a beam of 36ft, was not so lucky. Steindorff hit her in the port side at 6.30 am off St. Catherine's Point. So unexpected was the attack that only three of the crew survived. *UC-71* survived the war only to "founder" off Heligoland on the way to surrender on February 20, 1919.

The *Espagne*, built in 1909, now sits upright four metres high off the gravel seabed, and is well broken.

Yarmouth 19 miles; Lymington 21 miles.

220 Unknown. At 50 37 56; 01 27 10. Depth: 10m. The remains of this old cargo steamer can be found in this position in shallow water. The ship appears to have grounded stern first on to the Brook Ledges ¾ mile off Sudmore Point. The highest part of the wreck is the boiler, and there are some of her deck planks still in place. There is a large winch at the south-western end of the wreck.

Yarmouth 10 miles; Lymington 12 miles.

Area information and services

See Areas 1 and 5.

Shipwreck Register

This is a list of ships lost within the area covered by this book. They are listed by year of loss, name, and approximate position where known. Wrecks covered in the main text, have the site number included.

Ships known to have been salvaged after sinking or stranding, and vessels under 50 tons have not been included. This is, of course, not a complete list of every shipwreck in the area.

YEAR	NAME	LOCATION
1280	Just	Unknown
1301	Ship from Calais	Compton
1304	Mariote de Portsmouth	Solent
1313	St Mary of Bayonne	Atherfield
1315	Un-named	Grange Chine
1320	St Mary of Santander	Nr Yarmouth
	Un-named	Hanover
	Ralph de Georges Petition	Unknown
1335	Foreign ship	Unknown
1336	Ship of Jesus Christ	Unknown
1341	Spanish ship	Unknown
1375	Maudeleyn	Unknown
1399	A Breton ship	Unknown
1409	A Carrack from Italy	Needles
1439	Grace Dieu	Hamble River
1447	A Carrack	Unknown
1463	La Maudeleyn	Unknown
1544	Conception of Gastric	Unknown
1545	Mary Rose	69
1587	Michealmas	Unknown
1610	Un-named	Hanover
1627	Vliegende Dracke	Alum Bay
1627	Campen	16
1628	Campion	Unknown
1636	Bird Phoenix	Compton
1670	Un-named	Hanover
1691	St Anthony	Scratchells Bay
1695	Shark	Sandown Bay
1697	Un-named	Nr Cowes
1701	Dutch vessel	Atherfield
1701	Dutch vessel	Niton
1704	Un-named	Bembridge Ledge
1704	Un-named	Atherfield
1704	Un-named	Sandown Bay
1704	Un-named	Dunnose Point
1704	Un-named	Ventnor
1704	Un-named	St. Catherines
1704	Un-named	Chale Bay
1704	Un-named	Brook
1704	Dutch Fly Boat	Chilton
1704	Un-named	High Cliff
1705	HMS Looe	Needles
1711	Edgar	Spithead

YEAR	NAME	LOCATION
1743	Maria	Sandown Bay
1743	St. Dominic	Sandown Bay
1743	Success	Sandown Bay
1743	Curten	Ryde
1746	Dutch vessel	Chale
1746	English Ship	Cliff End
1746	Un-named	Totland
1746	Un-named	Ryde
1747	Marshall	Ryde
1748	Providence	Ryde
1749	Un-named	Chilton
1749	A Sloop	Brighstone
1749	Pretty Patsy	Bembridge
1750	St. Johannes	Off Island
1750	A Brig	Atherfield
1750	An English Ship	Typit Ledge
1750	Jonge Hans Gerten	Brook
1750	Warren	Grange
1750	Speedwell	Atherfield
1750	St. Johann	Atherfield
1751	Paul Catherine	Needles
1751	A Galliot	Brook
1751	Catherina	Totland
1752	4 Ships	Bembridge Ledge
1752	A Sloop	Watershoot
1752	Un-named	St. Catherines
1753	De Liefre	Cowes
1753	Un-named	East Solent
1753	A Dogger	Walpen Heath
1753	A Snow	St. Catherines
1753	A Ship	Atherfield
1753	Suspension of Arms	Ryde
1753	Deakins and Maudsley	Dunnose Point
1753	Friendship	Dunnose Point
1753	Deacons	St. Catherines
1753	Swanholm	Atherfield
1753	Dragon	Atherfield
1753	Dutch Vessel	Chilton
1753	A Brig	Compton
1753	4 Ships	High Cliff
1753	HMS Assurance	15
1753	Un-named	Needles
1754	Sandwich	Chale Bay
1754	Sandwisk	Atherfield
1754	A Snow	Compton
1754	A Brig	Ladder Chine
1754	French Sloop	Typit
1754	A Snow	Typit
1754	A Brig	Compton
1754	French Ketch	Brighstone
1754	A Brig	Atherfield
1754	Mary Anne	Chilton
1754	Diana	Hanover
1754	Hambro	Brighstone
1755	Watershoot	Off Island
1755	Lee	Barnes

YEAR	NAME	LOCATION
1755	A Snow	Barnes
1755	French Sloop	Compton
1755	Large Snow	Unknown
1755	A Sloop	Watershoot
1755	A Snow	St. Catherines
1755	Samuel	Brook
1755	St. Peter of Dieppe	Hanover
1755	Ann	Ventnor
1755	Un-named	St. Catherines
1756	Atwood	Atherfield
1756	A Ship	Typit
1756	Diane	Off Island
1757	Prince George	Needles
1757	A Galliot	Brighstone
1757	Jonge Bonne	Chilton
1757	A Collier	Ventnor
1757	Young Abraham	Atherfield
1757	Seahorse	Niton
1758	Cyprus	Barnes
1758	A Snow	Brook
1758	Faithful	Yarmouth
1758	HMS Invincible	95
1758	Alcyde	Scratchells Bay
1759	St. Vincent Ferrier	Unknown
1759	Spanish Snow	Atherfield
1759	Dutch Ship	Swingwill Ledge
1760	Hey	Brook
1760	Bluebell	Atherfield
1760	French Cutter	Sudmore
1760	Henry	Totland
1760	Jonge Arnoldus	Totland
1760	French Vessel	Totland
1760	Vries Van Leuwaarden	High Cliff
1760	Elizabeth	Chale Bay
1760	Koorn Bears	Bembridge Ledge
1762	Dutch Galliot	Cowlease Chine
1763	Voortfigtigheijd	Gurnard
1764	Dutch West Indiaman	Ryde
1764	Young Hendrick	Niton
1765	San Miguele	Barnes
1765	Apthorp	Scratchells Bay
1765	St. Michael	Watershoot
1766	Susanna	Atherfield
1766	English Snow	Compton
1766	French Sloop	Freshwater Gate
1766	Dutch Galliot	Atherfield
1766	Jonge Brother Parrenger	Back of Wight
1767	James or Jean	Chale Bay
1767	James	Hanover
1767	Three Friends	High Cliff
1769	Bergetha and Maria	Back of Wight
1769	A Brig	Atherfield
1769	A Sloop	St. Lawrence
1769	Katherine	Unknown
1769	Phoenix	Off Island
1769	Two Brothers	Back of Wight

YEAR	NAME	LOCATION
1770	North Star	Brook
1770	North Star of Hamburg	St. Catherines
1770	Dutch Ship	Sudmore
1770	King George	Unknown
1771	Edward	Unknown
1771	A Ship	Atherfield
1771	Edward Althorpe	Atherfield
1772	A Ship	Atherfield
1773	Conway	Needles
1774	Philicay Racket	Needles
1774	Philadelphia	Needles
1774	Morning Star	Atherfield
1775	Middleburgh Hope	Back of Wight
1775	A Ship	Atherfield
1775	Martin	Freshwater Bay
1776	Britania	Niton
1777	Ascension	Ryde
1777	Vrow Dorothea	Atherfield
1778	A Cutter	Brighstone
1778	Dutch Galliot Hoy	Freshwater Gate
1778	A Ship	Brighstone
1779	A Snow	Atherfield
1779	A Letter of Marque	Typit
1779	A Ship	High Cliff
1779	Portugese Schooner	Atherfield
1780	Incendiary	East Solent
1780	How	Chale Bay
1780	Berion Zues	Back of Wight
1781	Roberts	Scratchells Bay
1781	A Sloop	Brighstone
1782	HMS Royal George	73
1783	Jonna	St. Catherines
1783	A Kings Cutter	Brighstone
1783	A Brig	Barnes
1783	English Brig	Bembridge Ledge
1783	Dutch Sloop	Luccombe
1783	Danish Ship	Unknown
1783	Swan	Back of Wight
1784	Independance	Atherfield
1784	Juanna	St. Catherines
1784	English Cutter	Sudmore
1784	Friendship	Atherfield
1784	Earl of Cornwallis	St. Catherines
1785	Woohlsaart	Chale Bay
1785	Juenne Dragon	Nettlestone
1785	Dutch Brig	Undercliff
1785	French Brig	Undercliff
1785	A Galliot	Typit
1785	Marchent	Atherfield
1785	Jussrow Anna Louisa	Atherfield
1785	Dorothea Charlotte	Compton
1786	Juno	194
1786	French Brig	Old Node
1786	La Maria	High Cliff
1786	James	Chale
1786	James Ryder	Niton

YEAR	NAME	LOCATION
1789	French Sloop	Atherfield
1790	William and Mary	Off Island
1790	Good Intent	Ryde
1791	Weymouth	St. Catherines
1791	A Hoy	Niton
1791	A Brig	Brook
1791	Small Cutter	Atherfield
1792	Dutch Ship	Grange
1792	Dolphin	Atherfield
1792	A Sloop	Typit
1793	Harvey	Chale Bay
1793	Vrow Anna Maria	Ventnor
1793	St George	Niton
1793	Countess Hoberton	Needles
1793	Garland	Hanover
1793	Kinds Increase	St. Catherines
1794	General Clark	Brook
1794	Bolton	Atherfield
1794	Juno	St. Catherines
1794	English Brig	Southmore
1794	Ann	Yarmouth
1795	Friends Increase	Niton
1795	Small Spaniard	Southmore
1795	Alexander	Chale
1795	Nia Srad' Etal	Niton
1795	Emeralos	Ventnor
1795	A Hoy	Brighstone
1795	Boyne	68
1796	A Brig	Sandown Fort
1796	Fair Mag	Bembridge
1797	Buona Elina	Brook
1798	Gute Entwarting	High Cliff
1798	Henry Addington	Bembridge
1798	A Snow	Atherfield
1799	Guernsey Lilly	Yarmouth
1799	Dorothea Elizabeth	Ventnor
1799	Three Sisters	Ventnor
1799	Thetis	Sandown Bay
1799	HMS Deux Amies	Grange Chine
1799	HMS Impregnable	94
1799	A Collier	Bembridge Ledge
1799	A Schooner	Grange
1799	A Hoy	Atherfield
1799	Britania Forbes	West Solent
1799	Betsy Thompson	Yarmouth
1800	Henri Et Loutuil	Back of Wight
1800	Therapsy	Ladder Chine
1801	East Countryman	Atherfield
1801	Scout	Shingle Bank
1803	Aururo Van Farrer	Osborne Bay
1803	A Schooner	Chale
1803	A Hoy	St. Catherines
1803	A Schooner	Sudmore
1803	Hindostan	Culver Cliff
1803	Caton Bleche	Sandown Bay
1804	HMS Hannibal	Sandown Fort

YEAR	NAME	LOCATION
1808	Transport Ship	St. Catherines
1811	HMS Pommone	15
1813	Good Advice	Chilton
1814	Salome	Westend Point
1818	Pilgrim	Needles
1818	Speculator	Sandown Bay
1818	Somerset	Yarmouth
1821	Herman	Off Island
1823	Le Courier	St. Catherines
1829	Carn Brae Castle	Brook
1829	HMS Nightingale	Shingle Bank
1830	Stephanotis	Unknown
1830	Research	Back of Wight
1830	Rosine	Atherfield
1830	Cameo	Unknown
1830	Diane Faur	Totland
1830	Moland	Brook
1831	Julie	Yarmouth
1831	Bainsbridge	Atherfield
1832	Crosique	Chale
1832	Charles II	Sandown Bay
1833	Henrye	Sandown Bay
1833	Blessington	Freshwater Bay
1835	Providence	Niton
1836	Clarendon	Chale
1837	Jean Maria	Chale
1838	Dream	15
1838	Enighden	Chale
1838	Claire	Brook
1840	Castor	Chale
1840	Edgar	Unknown
1841	Castor	Sandown Bay
1841	Dover	Freshwater Bay
1841	Mary Ann	Freshwater Bay
1842	Kent	Shingle Bank
1842	Mary Coxon	Nettlestone
1842	Lively	Bembridge
1843	George	Atherfield
1845	Siam	Hanover
1846	HMS Sphinx	Chale
1846	Ann and Elizabeth	Spithead
1847	Perdoitus	St. Catherines
1848	Llanrumney	Atherfield
1848	Ann	Back of Wight
1850	Tale Banre	Sandown Bay
1851	Ocean	Yarmouth
1851	Perlen	Freshwater Bay
1851	Vivid	Cowes
1852	Constant James	Chale
1852	St. Barbe	Needles
1852	Tjsemboelvert	Needles
1853	Navarino	St. Catherines
1853	Hibernia	Bonchurch
1856	Cashmere	St. Catherines
1856	Mars	Atherfield
1856	Mathilde	Atherfield

YEAR	NAME	LOCATION
1857	Temerario	Chilton
1857	Redport	Back of Wight
1858	Abbey Langdon	Compton
1859	Lelia	St. Catherines
1859	Jane	St. Catherines
1859	Mirabita	Chilton
1859	Sentinel	Brook
1861	John Wesley	Compton
1861	Victor Emmanuel	Chale
1861	Corsair	Bonchurch
1862	Helen Horsfall	Brighstone
1862	Cedarine	Chilton
1862	Lotus	St. Catherines
1863	Three Sisters	Chale
1863	Chancellor	138
1864	Rambler	Unknown
1864	Thetis	St. Catherines
1865	Lucy	Unknown
1865	Jesper	Bembridge
1866	Sauvegarde	Unknown
1866	Fahli Bure	Sandown Bay
1867	Fortuna	Atherfield
1867	Johannes	St. Catherines
1868	C.B.	Atherfield
1869	Magellen	Totland
1869	Rio De Janerio	Back of Wight
1870	Don Quixhotte	Sandown Bay
1870	See Bee	High Cliff
1870	Normandy	Off the Isle of Wight
1871	Underley	168
1871	Vallid	St. Catherines
1871	Catharina	Unknown
1871	Anna	Grange
1871	Cassandra	Brook
1872	L'Etoile	Sudmore
1872	Malcolm Brown	Compton
1872	Hope	Freshwater Bay
1872	Dacca	St. Catherines
1873	Sisters	Atherfield
1873	Vallid of Androssan	St. Catherines
1873	Quail	Grange
1873	Woodham	Grange
1874	Hermose Habanero	Sudmore
1875	Newbiggin	Atherfield
1875	Mistletoe	Stokes Bay
1875	Pirro	Sandown Bay
1875	Robert	Cowes
1876	Glenary	St. Catherines
1877	Two Brothers	East Solent
1877	Batistina	Warden Ledge
1877	Champion	Shingle Bank
1877	Cloud	Niton
1877	Alpheta	Bembridge Ledge
1877	John Douse	Sandown Bay
1878	Manora	Sandown Bay
1878	St. Etienne	Warden Ledge

YEAR	NAME	LOCATION
1879	Alpheus Marshall	Atherfield
1879	Mignonette	Brook
1879	Schiehallion	St. Catherines
1879	Stemman	St. Catherines
1880	Atlas	Atherfield
1880	Joseph and Mary	Brook
1880	Providence	Spithead
1880	Blanche	Nettlestone
1880	Sea Plover	Nettlestone
1880	Donna Zola	Atherfield
1881	Essen	St. Catherines
1881	Caduceus	108
1881	Providence	Totland
1881	Arrow	Cowes
1881	Indian Chief	Not known
1881	Gertrude	Ryde
1881	Eclipse	Ryde
1881	Lucknow	Ryde
1881	Tartar	Nettlestone
1881	Alarm	Off Island
1881	Claremont	Chale
1882	Wheatfield	St. Catherines
1883	Georges Henri	St. Catherines
1883	Foam	Totland
1883	Jeune Gustan	Sandown Bay
1883	Mogellen	Needles
1883	Jane	Cowes
1883	Castle Craig	Brook
1883	Hero	Niton
1883	Beau Monde	St. Catherines
1884	Commodore	St. Catherines
1884	Simla	Needles
1884	Etoile De La Mer	Sandown Bay
1885	Flirt	St. Catherines
1885	Perseverence	Sandown Bay
1886	Comorant	Atherfield
1886	Britons Queen	Bembridge
1886	Fleur De Lis	Cowes
1886	Mexico	—
1887	Medway	Yarmouth
1887	Pride of The Sea	Sandown Bay
1888	Sirenia	Atherfield
1888	Friends	Ryde
1888	Konseg	St. Catherines
1889	Isle of Cyprus	Off Island
1889	Cleddy	St. Catherines
1890	Dizzy Dunlop	Atherfield
1890	Jeanne Benoni	St. Catherines
1890	Henri Leontine	Brook
1890	Caboceen	Brook
1890	Cameo	Brook
1890	Irex	17
1890	Tyne	Off Island
1892	Walmer Castle	Back of Wight
1892	Combury Castle	Ventnor
1892	Vectis	Totland

YEAR	NAME	LOCATION
1892	Catan	Unknown
1892	Gudrun	Shingle Bank
1893	R.T.C. No 9	57
1893	Gripfast	Unknown
1894	Volzy	Back of Wight
1895	Spree	Unknown
1895	Noordster	Off Island
1895	Ganymedes	Shingle Bank
1896	Johaus Millas	Grange
1897	Emma	Off Island
1897	Alcester	Atherfield
1898	Ernst	Shingle Bank
1898	Mathilde	St. Catherines
1898	Rosalie	Bembridge
1899	Moland	Barnes
1899	Midge	East Solent
1900	Iduna	216
1900	Atlas	Atherfield
1900	Auguste	195
1900	Matilde	Off Island
1900	San Sebastian	Off Island
1901	Plover	Ryde
1901	Slator	Niton
1901	Cid	Cowes
1902	Russie	St. Catherines
1903	Trixie	East Solent
1903	Violet	Ryde
1903	Cymric	Off Island
1903	Slater	Back of Wight
1903	Eira	Ryde
1903	Dodo	Ryde
1903	Cuckoo	Ryde
1904	The Saint	Warden Ledge
1904	Dolly	Atherfield
1905	Ino	East Solent
1905	St. Monan	Atherfield
1905	Albatross	West Solent
1905	Glorie De Marie	Dunnose
1905	Satyr	Brook
1906	Firefly	St. Catherines
1906	HMS Mars	Needles
1906	Anita	Unknown
1906	Briton	Chilton
1906	Dolores	St. Catherines
1907	Berlin	Off Island
1907	Snevic	Off Island
1907	Reindeer	22
1908	Cayo Soto	Unknown
1909	Withern	87
1909	William and Mary of Maldon	Brighstone
1910	Rene	Watcombe Bay
1910	Nemrod	St. Catherines
1910	Monte Grande	Off Island
1911	HMS A1 (target)	109
1912	Prim	Sudmore
1913	Maggie III	Off Island

DIVE WIGHT AND HAMPSHIRE

YEAR	NAME	LOCATION
1914	Neath	Cowes
1914	Balder	Freshwater Bay
1914	Ida	Whitecliff Bay
1915	Louis	Off Island
1915	Resource II	Southampton
1915	Erin II	Nab Tower
1915	Star of Buchan	Nab Tower
1915	HMS Velox	117
1916	Charlotte Sophia	Nodes Point
1916	Empress Queen	130
1916	Albion II	St. Catherines
1916	Pelagia	Nab Tower
1916	Algerian	45
1916	Hendrick	Off Island
1916	Souvenir	Brook
1917	Camberwell	181
1917	Osaki	Unknown
1917	Myrtle Grove	Off Needles
1917	Westville	199
1917	Espagne	219
1917	Oriflamme	196
1917	Fallodon	187
1917	Camswan	150
1917	Apley	156
1917	U.B. 81	184
1917	Luciston	48
1917	Wapello	182
1917	Lucknow	Portsmouth
1917	Ocean Star	Nab Tower
1917	M.L. 62	Sandown Bay
1917	Florence Louisa	Needles
1917	Elford	153
1917	Mendi	213
1917	Brigitta	Nab Tower
1917	Redesmere	208
1917	Ada	Ryde
1918	Mechanician	8
1918	War Knight	193
1918	Serrana	6 & 12
1918	Azzemour	24
1918	Braat II	212
1918	Tweed	214
1918	Londonier	210
1918	Isleworth	179
1918	Asborg	180
1918	Polo	169
1918	Luis	167
1918	Highland Brigade	183
1918	Leon	170
1918	HMS Boxer	151
1918	France Aimee	128
1918	HMS Hazard	98
1918	South Western	217
1918	HMS P12	131 & 141
1918	Eleanor	Needles
1918	Michael Clements	St. Catherines

YEAR	NAME	LOCATION
1918	New Dawn	Needles
1918	Molina	210
1918	Borgny	23
1919	Violet	Bembridge
1919	Walcutta	Off Island
1919	Edward Luckenbach	Unknown
1919	Scotch Dyke	Off Island
1920	Heardsman	Off Island
1920	HMS Liffey	Off Island
1920	U.B. 21	105
1921	Lois	Chale
1921	Imogen	Shingle Bank
1921	Coastal Motor Boat	Unknown
1921	SMS Baden (German)	178
1922	Pearl	81
1924	Duddon (lighter)	66
1928	HMS Undine	East Solent
1932	Rainbow	Off Island
1939	H.M.T. Warick Deeping	St. Catherines
1940	HMS Swordfish	190
1940	Crestflower	211
1940	Capable	113
1940	Cambrian	91
1940	Campeador 5	133 & 121
1940	'E' Boat	116
1940	HMS Acheron	207
1940	Charde	Portsmouth
1940	James No 70	Southampton
1940	Bonaparte	Southampton
1940	P.S. Her Majesty	Southampton
1940	Ajax	26
1940	Coquetdale	25
1940	Terlings	28
1940	HMS Kingston Cairngorm	Not given
1940	Kolske 6	Unknown
1940	Islay Mist	Watcombe Bay
1941	Portsdown (paddle steamer)	Southsea
1941	Irishman (tug)	86
1943	Kingston Jacinth	Portsmouth
1943	Sargasso	Unknown
1943	Landing Craft 553	Southampton
1943	Landing Craft 136	Southampton
1943	Landing Craft 17	Unknown
1944	Dungrange	St. Catherines
1944	Ashanti	209
1944	LCT529	132
1944	Flying Boat	31
1944	Gentrice	St. Catherines
1944	Landing Craft 541	Off Island
1944	Landing Craft 52	Off Island
1944	Landing Craft 895	Portsmouth
1944	Landing Craft 801	Portsmouth
1944	Landing Craft 1199	Portsmouth
1944	Landing Craft 154	Portsmouth
1944	LCT 809	7
1944	Minora	Not given

YEAR	NAME	LOCATION
1944	Cuba	162
1944	U1195	175
1944	Swarthy	Off Island
1947	Varvassi	18
1947	LCT 1068	58
1948	Hope	Chale
1951	Volkerak	St. Catherines
1952	Albatross	St. Catherines
1956	Priscilla (tug)	Compton
1957	HMS Upstart (target)	205
1964	Witte Zee	202
1967	Roway	82
1967	Tenance	174
1968	Bettann	126 & 160
1970	Harry Sharman	140
1973	Hauler	139
1975	Estrelita	147
1975	Piper Aircraft	164
1976	Chain Ferry	49
1978	Margaret Smith	41
1978	M.F.V. New Venture	143
1979	Pool Fisher	206
1980	Barge	9

Index